Eyewitness
NATURAL DISASTERS

Buddhist statue
survives tsunami

Optical telescope scans
space for asteroids

Fire engine

Doppler
radar dome

Track buckled
by giant wave

Eyewitness
NATURAL DISASTERS

Hurricane-warning
flags

Written by
CLAIRE WATTS

Consultant
TREVOR DAY

Spirit of
Smallpox carving

Planet Earth

Seismograph

Body casts,
Pompeii

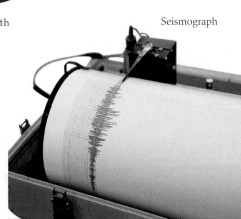

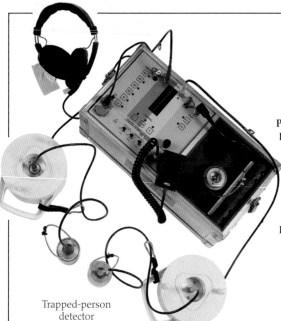

Trapped-person detector

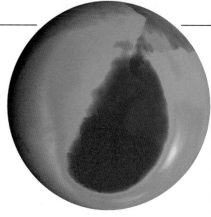

Ozone hole over Antarctica

LONDON, NEW YORK, MELBOURNE, MUNICH, and DELHI

Project editors Jackie Fortey and Carey Scott
Designers Johnny Pau, Samantha Richiardi
Senior designer Owen Peyton-Jones
Managing editor Camilla Hallinan
Managing art editor Sophia M. Tampakopoulos
Publishing managers Caroline Buckingham,
Andrew Macintyre
Category publisher Laura Buller
Production controller Gordana Simakovic
Picture researchers Celia Dearing,
Julia Harris-Voss, and Jo Walton
DK picture library Rose Horridge
DTP designer Andy Hilliard
Jacket designer Sarah Ponder

REVISED EDITION

Revised by John Woodward

DK INDIA
Project editor Nidhi Sharma
Project art editor Rajnish Kashyap
Editor Pallavi Singh
Designer Honlung Zach Ragui
Managing editor Saloni Talwar
Managing art editor Romi Chakraborty
DTP designer Tarun Sharma
Picture researcher Sumedha Chopra

DK UK
Senior editor Rob Houston
Senior art editor Philip Letsu
Production editor Adam Stoneham
Production controller Rebecca Short
Publisher Andrew Macintyre

DK US
US editor Margaret Parrish
Editorial director Nancy Ellwood

Revised edition published in the United States in 2012
by DK Publishing, 375 Hudson Street, New York, New York 10014
First published in the United States in 2006

10 9 8 7 6 5 4 3 2 1
001—183529—Jul/12

Tsunami warning buoy

Mayan rain god

DK books are available at special discounts when purchased in
bulk for sales promotions, premiums, fundraising, or educational use.
For details, contact: DK Publishing Special Markets
375 Hudson Street, New York, New York 10014
SpecialSales@dk.com

A catalog record for this book is available from the Library of Congress.

ISBN: 978-0-7566-9302-2 (Hardcover)
ISBN: 978-0-7566-9303-9 (ALB)

Color reproduction by Colourscan, Singapore
Printed and bound in China
by Toppan Printing Co. (Shenzhen) Ltd.

Hokusai's
Great Wave
painting

Discover more at
www.dk.com

Smokejumper

Contents

Lava fountains erupt from
Mount Etna

Dynamic planet

PLANET EARTH provides us with the air, food, warmth, and the materials we need to thrive. But Earth can also generate catastrophic disasters, from tsunamis and landslides to tornadoes and wildfires, that take lives, damage the environment, destroy property, and disrupt normal life. Such disasters may be sudden and violent, such as an earthquake or flood, or gradual, like a drought or the spread of a deadly disease. Today, scientists have shown that many such disasters are caused by the natural workings of our planet. There are more than 700 natural disasters every year, affecting around one person in 30.

TSUNAMI STRIKES LISBON
This picture of the 1755 earthquake and tsunami that destroyed Portugal's capital Lisbon shows buildings leaning at impossible angles. Before today's instant news media, and before photography, facts and images were often exaggerated.

RESTLESS PLANET
The way the Earth behaves is controlled by the Sun and by the inner workings of the planet itself. Energy from the Sun drives the weather, and is the source of disasters, including extreme events such as droughts, floods, and hurricanes. Heat from within the Earth causes movement of the rocks beneath us, which can lead to earthquakes, volcanoes, and tsunamis.

Land heaved upward, leaving this house at a precarious angle

RIVERS OF LAVA
Fiery torrents of lava spew out of Kilauea, in Hawaii. Kilauea is one of the most active volcanoes in the world, erupting almost constantly. There are more than 1,000 active volcanoes on land today—surface signs of the immense pressures and high temperatures deep below the ground.

DEVASTATING EARTHQUAKES
Earthquakes are among the most feared of all natural disasters. This street in Ojiya City, northern Japan was turned on its side following a quake in October 2004. During the 20th century, there were almost 1.5 million deaths from earthquakes and, as the world's population grows, earthquake fatalities are likely to increase. In October 2005, a single quake killed 38,000 in Pakistan. Survivors of earthquakes are frequently left with nothing but the clothes on their backs, as buildings collapse and transportation links, electricity, water supplies, and telephone links are cut. Essential services, such as hospitals, may not be able to operate normally. People can lose their livelihoods, too, as farms, factories, and offices are ripped apart.

BLAZING FORESTS

Wildfires, such as this one which struck Big Sur, California, may be ignited by lightning, or by someone dropping a match. They can destroy hundreds of acres of fertile forest, leaving a scarred and seemingly lifeless landscape. However, the damage they cause is only temporary. The forest has the natural ability to regenerate itself gradually. But if the wind blows the fire toward an urban area, buildings and people's lives may be at risk from the oncoming flames and the clouds of choking smoke.

*New growth
as first rainfall
germinates seeds*

A DRY WORLD

As the world's population grows, so the demand for water increases. Evidence suggests that human activities such as cutting down forests are changing local weather patterns, making droughts more likely. More than 100 million people in over 20 countries in Africa, Central Asia, and South America currently suffer the effects of drought.

DEADLY DISEASES

Most diseases that cause widespread illness and death come from microscopic organisms, such as the malaria-carrying parasite that lives in the saliva of mosquitoes. Forty percent of the world's population lives in areas where there is a high risk of being infected with malaria. Attempts to eradicate the disease and to create a vaccine have so far been unsuccessful. Malaria continues to kill more than one million people every year.

*Piercing mouthparts
for drawing blood*

*Residents carry their
possessions as they
flee the dangers of
the erupting volcano*

ESCAPE

In 1984, 73,000 people were evacuated from their homes around the Mayon volcano in the Philippines. Scientists monitoring the volcano's activity had been able to predict a coming eruption. Modern technology, such as satellites, which help meteorologists to produce accurate weather forecasts, makes it possible to detect major disasters, giving people time to prepare for the crisis.

Restless Earth

DEEP INSIDE THE EARTH, temperatures and pressures are so great that they can transform carbon deposits into diamond—the hardest of all minerals. The Earth's surface, or crust, is divided into massive slabs called tectonic plates. Some of the plates are crunching together, some drifting apart, while others grind past each other. The intense heat and pressure inside the Earth disturb the tectonic plates. When released at the Earth's surface, the pressure and heat can cause earthquakes, volcanoes, and tsunamis. This can have devastating consequences, particularly for regions close to the edges of the tectonic plates.

Diamond embedded in volcanic rock

South America and Africa fitted together

Atlantic Ocean now separates South America and Africa

PANGAEA
The plates that make up the Earth's surface have been moving and changing shape ever since they formed, at least 3.6 billion years ago, bringing continents together and splitting them apart. Around 200 million years ago, at the time of the dinosaurs, all the continents were part of one landmass known as Pangaea.

THE EARTH TODAY
Over the last 200 million years, the tectonic plates between Europe and the Americas have moved apart, opening up the Atlantic Ocean. Each year, the continents shift by nearly half an inch (at least 1 cm), in some cases much more than this. In another 200 million years, the map will look different again.

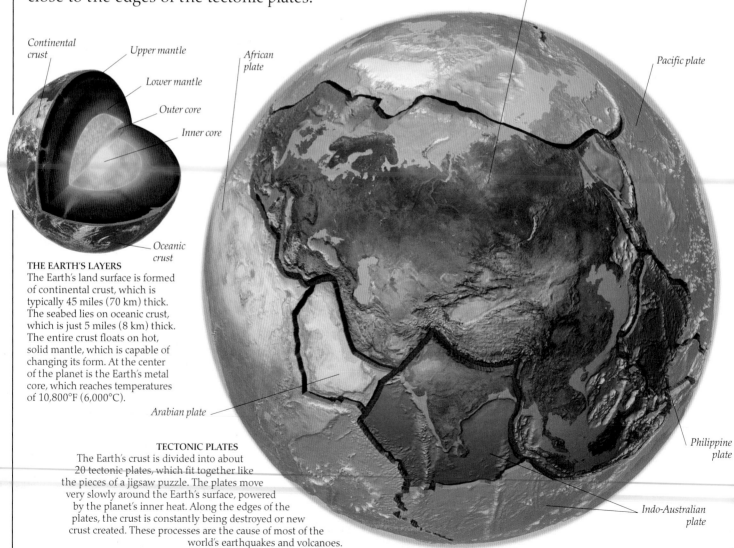

Continental crust
Upper mantle
Lower mantle
Outer core
Inner core
Oceanic crust

African plate
Eurasian plate
Pacific plate
Arabian plate
Philippine plate
Indo-Australian plate

THE EARTH'S LAYERS
The Earth's land surface is formed of continental crust, which is typically 45 miles (70 km) thick. The seabed lies on oceanic crust, which is just 5 miles (8 km) thick. The entire crust floats on hot, solid mantle, which is capable of changing its form. At the center of the planet is the Earth's metal core, which reaches temperatures of 10,800°F (6,000°C).

TECTONIC PLATES
The Earth's crust is divided into about 20 tectonic plates, which fit together like the pieces of a jigsaw puzzle. The plates move very slowly around the Earth's surface, powered by the planet's inner heat. Along the edges of the plates, the crust is constantly being destroyed or new crust created. These processes are the cause of most of the world's earthquakes and volcanoes.

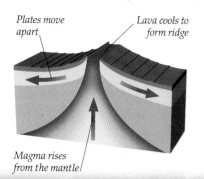

Plates move apart

Lava cools to form ridge

Magma rises from the mantle

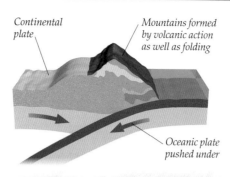

Continental plate

Mountains formed by volcanic action as well as folding

Oceanic plate pushed under

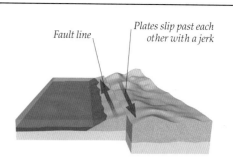

Fault line

Plates slip past each other with a jerk

DIVERGENT BOUNDARY

When plates move apart, or diverge, new crust is formed by molten rock rising into the gap. Along the middle of the Red Sea and its right-hand arm, the Gulf of Aqaba, the African and Arabian plates have been diverging for 50 million years. Most divergent boundaries in oceans form ocean ridges, such as the Mid-Atlantic Ridge.

CONVERGENT BOUNDARY

When an oceanic plate moves toward, or converges with, a continental plate, the oceanic plate is pushed down (subducted) beneath the continental plate, creating a steep-sided trench in the ocean floor. The subducted crust melts into magma, which then rises through the continental crust to form a volcanic mountain range, such as the Andes in South America, which is peppered with volcanoes.

TRANSFORM FAULT

The place where two plates slide past each other is called a transform fault, such as the San Andreas Fault on the Pacific coast of the US. Friction between the rocks may make the plates jam. Gradually, pressure builds up until the plates slip past each other with a violent jerk, causing an earthquake or triggering a tsunami.

NEW CRUST

Wherever magma (molten rock) emerges from the Earth's mantle, new crust is created. This may happen in a violent volcanic eruption or, more gently, as the plates diverge. Magma also leaks through weak points in the Earth's crust at hot spots far from the plate boundaries. As the plate moves gradually over the hot spot, the magma—called lava once it reaches the surface—may form a chain of volcanic islands, such as the Hawaiian or Galápagos islands. This view from the air shows lava from Kilauea volcano on Hawaii flowing into the Pacific Ocean.

As lava cools it hardens into rock

Steam rises as hot lava flows into the sea

The Earth shakes

T HE SURFACE OF OUR PLANET seems solid and unmoving—but the Earth's plates are moving all the time, sometimes gently and gradually, and sometimes with a sudden jolt that makes the ground shake. Earthquakes are usually measured using a scale devised in 1935 by Charles Richter. The smallest recorded quakes measure up to 3.5 on the Richter scale, a degree of ground movement that may be just enough to rattle a cup on a table. The most severe earthquakes measure over 8 and can destroy entire cities. Earthquakes cannot be prevented, but scientists can study the records of past quakes and measure the build-up of stresses within the rocks. Then, they can forecast the probability of a substantial earthquake happening within a certain time.

POSEIDON THE EARTH SHAKER
In ancient Greece, people believed that earthquakes were caused by the god of the sea, Poseidon. When he was angry, Poseidon stamped on the ground or struck the Earth with his three-pronged trident, and set off an earthquake. His unpredictable, violent behavior earned Poseidon the nickname Earth-Shaker.

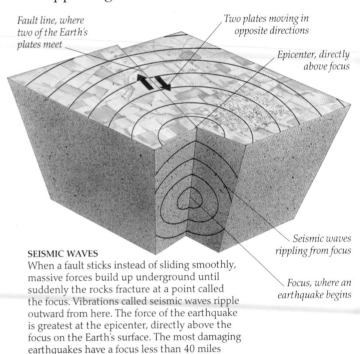

Fault line, where two of the Earth's plates meet

Two plates moving in opposite directions

Epicenter, directly above focus

Seismic waves rippling from focus

Focus, where an earthquake begins

SEISMIC WAVES
When a fault sticks instead of sliding smoothly, massive forces build up underground until suddenly the rocks fracture at a point called the focus. Vibrations called seismic waves ripple outward from here. The force of the earthquake is greatest at the epicenter, directly above the focus on the Earth's surface. The most damaging earthquakes have a focus less than 40 miles (65 km) beneath the Earth's surface.

SAN ANDREAS FAULT
Like many fault lines, the San Andreas fault line generates many earthquakes. Extending 750 miles (1,207 km) through central California, it divides the Pacific and North American tectonic plates, and causes frequent earth tremors in the cities of San Francisco and Los Angeles. Some parts of the fault slip in regular jerks that produce slight tremors, while others get jammed and then shift as pressure is released, causing a major earthquake.

L.A. TRAFFIC JAMMED
An unusual pile-up happened when an earthquake measuring 6.7 struck Los Angeles on January 17, 1994. The lowest floor of a building settled onto the cars parked below, crushing them. There was also massive damage to other buildings, power supplies, roads, and a major dam. People who live along the San Andreas Fault are used to small tremors occurring almost daily, but larger earthquakes, such as this one, are rare.

HAITI QUAKE

When an earthquake measuring 7 hit the Caribbean island of Haiti on January 12, 2010, it devastated the poverty-stricken nation with no standards for building construction. Up to 250,000 houses and 30,000 commercial structures collapsed or were badly damaged, and nearly 100,000 people died—most of them crushed by collapsing buildings. Rescue efforts were hampered by a breakdown of communications, as well as about 54 aftershocks that brought down buildings already damaged by the main quake.

Epicenter of earthquake

Colored bands are narrow around the epicenter, showing greater land displacement

Fault line

EARTHQUAKE DETECTOR

In 132 CE, Chinese astronomer Zhang Heng invented the first seismoscope, a device for detecting ground movement. This bronze device shows the direction a tremor comes from, and works within a range of about 40 miles (65 km).

Earth tremors cause one of the dragons to release a ball

Ball falls into open mouth of toad below

Toad farthest from epicenter catches the ball. The quake lies in the opposite direction from that of the toad

GROUND MOVEMENTS

This satellite radar image shows movements of land following an earthquake measuring 7.1 in California in 1999. The colored bands represent contours. The distance between adjacent contours of the same color indicate 4 in (10 cm) of ground displacement.

The greater the shockwave, the wider the zigzag on the display

Fine needle moves with tremors, recording the vibrations with ink

REVEALING QUAKES

Earth tremors can be detected, recorded, and measured using a seismograph, such as this portable device. Seismographs can detect vibrations called foreshocks, which are produced by deep rocks fracturing before an earthquake. Monitoring foreshocks helps scientists to predict earthquakes.

Surviving a quake

ENGINEERS SAY that it is not earthquakes that kill, but buildings. Earthquakes usually have a minor impact in the wilderness, but when they affect built-up areas, the results can be devastating. In some earthquake zones, buildings are specially constructed to absorb vibrations without collapsing. But even supposedly earthquake-proof cities may come crashing down in a major quake. When an earthquake does strike, emergency plans are put into action. Trained teams are despatched to rescue the injured from the rubble, evacuate victims from danger zones, fight fires, make ruined buildings safe, and, eventually, restore essential services.

FIGHTING FIRE
After the ground has stopped shaking, damage to electrical equipment and gas pipes can lead to an outbreak of fires. Firefighters have to struggle through the ruined buildings and broken roads to reach the blaze. In Kobe, Japan, many of the city's ancient wooden buildings burned down when firefighters ran out of water.

CITY IN RUINS
The ancient fortress, or citadel, of Arg-e Bam stood on a hill overlooking the city of Bam in Iran for 11 centuries, until December 27, 2003. The violent earthquake that hit Bam that day flattened the modern city, as well as the mud-brick fortress and other historic buildings dating back to the 16th and 17th centuries. More than 26,000 people died and 70,000 were left homeless.

THE CITADEL OF ARG-E BAM IN 2003

THE CITADEL OF ARG-E BAM IN 2004

Shaking caused the loose ground to move like a liquid, and it could no longer support the freeway

SHOCK IN JAPAN
During the earthquake that struck the city of Kobe, Japan, on January 17, 1995, bolts holding together elevated (built above ground) roads snapped, sending sections of road crashing to the ground. Much of Kobe is built on ground that becomes unstable during an earthquake. Also, the epicenter of the 6.9 magnitude earthquake was only 12 miles (20 km) from the city. Its shockwaves damaged or destroyed some 140,000 buildings and claimed the lives of 5,500 people.

SEARCHING FOR LIFE
When an earthquake hits a city, people can be buried alive inside collapsed buildings. It is vital that rescuers find them quickly before they suffocate or die of their injuries, or perish from lack of water and food. Rescuers may use a trapped-person detector, like this one. The device can detect vibrations as faint as those from a heartbeat, letting rescuers know if anyone is alive in the rubble.

Earphones, for listening for signs of life

EMERGENCY SHELTER
An earthquake victim is given a medical check-up in an evacuation center. One month after Kobe's earthquake, 226,000 people were living in centers like this one. Some 300,000 people lost their homes and the authorities were unable to accommodate all of them. Some had to sleep in tents or in their cars in freezing winter weather.

Sensor, for picking up vibrations

Microphone, for amplifying sounds from vibrations

Freeway buckled when waves rippled across ground surface

Subsensors can be placed in different parts of a building

Cable coil, to enable sensors to be moved around so that every part of a building can be investigated

COMBING THE RUBBLE
Trained dogs can help rescue workers by sniffing out survivors in the rubble of a collapsed building. Dogs have the added advantage that they can move lightly over loose material, while a person's weight could disturb the rubble and cause more debris to fall on anyone trapped below.

What is a tsunami?

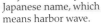

THE FIRST SIGN of a tsunami (soo-nah-mee) approaching the coast may be a sudden swell in the ocean, like the surge before a storm at sea. But a tsunami is no storm surge. Tsunamis are caused by massive shifts, or displacements, of water, usually due to movements of the seafloor that accompany undersea earthquakes. They are the deadliest of all waves. They can travel at speeds of 590 mph (950 kph) and, when they reach the shore, can be as high as 100 ft (30 m). A tsunami may not be just one wave, but a chain of waves, and the first is rarely the biggest. Massive walls of water can slam against the coast for hours, stripping sand away from beaches and tearing up trees and vegetation. The fast-moving water can sweep inland, flooding fields and wreaking havoc on towns and villages.

THE GREAT WAVE
This famous Japanese painting by Katsushika Hokusai shows a towering wave. Tsunamis used to be called tidal waves, but it is now known that they are not caused by tides. Today, they are called by their Japanese name, which means harbor wave.

LANDSLIDE
Tsunamis can be caused by massive landslides into the sea. As debris plunges into the water, the accompanying splash and sudden displacement of water can generate a violent tsunami. However, tsunamis started by landslides usually affect only the local area and quickly subside.

Soufrière Hills volcano, Monserrat, 1997

Clouds of smoke and ash cascading from Mount Pelée, Martinique

VOLCANIC ERUPTION
When Mount Pelée on the Caribbean island of Martinique erupted on May 7, 1902, the volcano sent out a torrent of volcanic gas, ash, and rock fragments called a pyroclastic flow. When this material fell into the sea, it caused a tsunami that devastated the island's harbor.

IMPACT FROM SPACE
Every day, hundreds of rocky objects fall from space. Most burn up in the atmosphere to become shooting stars. Those that reach Earth, such as this one, are called meteorites. Many land in the ocean and simply sink to the bottom. If a huge object—such as an asteroid—hits the ocean, its impact may cause a tsunami.

Meteorite composed of stone and iron

EARTHQUAKE
Most tsunamis are caused by earthquakes around the edges of the Earth's tectonic plates. When an earthquake strikes, huge cracks in the ground can open up, as in this salt marsh in Gujarat, India. When this occurs under the ocean, the shockwaves from the violent movement can cause a tsunami.

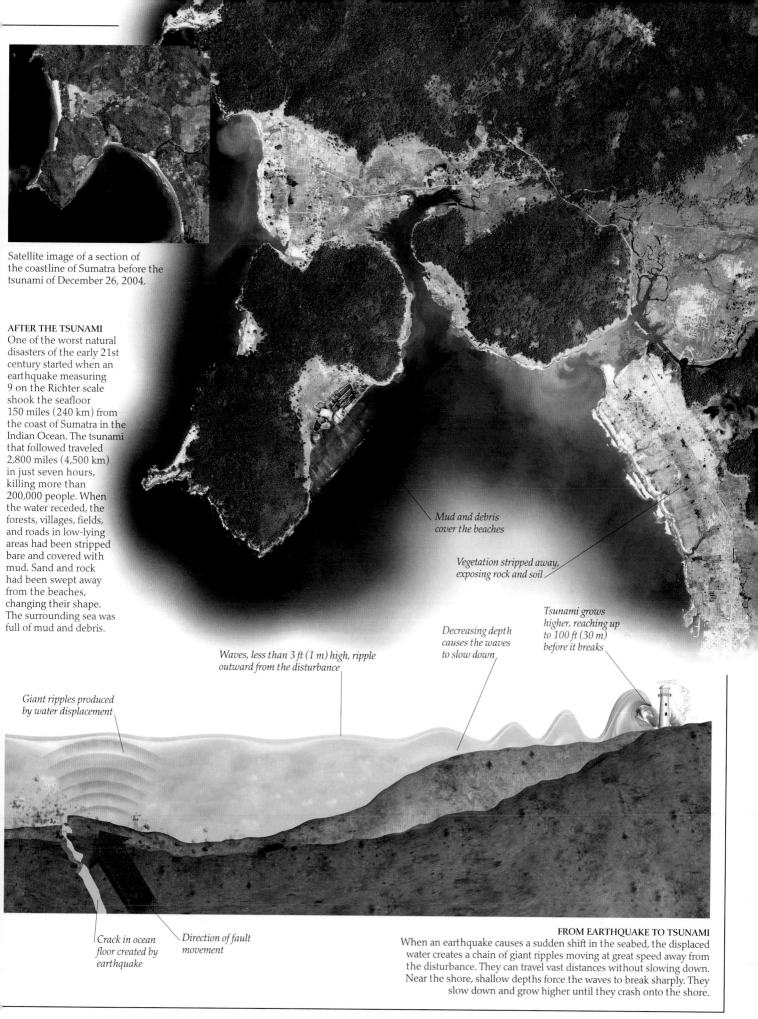

Satellite image of a section of the coastline of Sumatra before the tsunami of December 26, 2004.

AFTER THE TSUNAMI
One of the worst natural disasters of the early 21st century started when an earthquake measuring 9 on the Richter scale shook the seafloor 150 miles (240 km) from the coast of Sumatra in the Indian Ocean. The tsunami that followed traveled 2,800 miles (4,500 km) in just seven hours, killing more than 200,000 people. When the water receded, the forests, villages, fields, and roads in low-lying areas had been stripped bare and covered with mud. Sand and rock had been swept away from the beaches, changing their shape. The surrounding sea was full of mud and debris.

Mud and debris cover the beaches

Vegetation stripped away, exposing rock and soil

Tsunami grows higher, reaching up to 100 ft (30 m) before it breaks

Decreasing depth causes the waves to slow down

Waves, less than 3 ft (1 m) high, ripple outward from the disturbance

Giant ripples produced by water displacement

Crack in ocean floor created by earthquake

Direction of fault movement

FROM EARTHQUAKE TO TSUNAMI
When an earthquake causes a sudden shift in the seabed, the displaced water creates a chain of giant ripples moving at great speed away from the disturbance. They can travel vast distances without slowing down. Near the shore, shallow depths force the waves to break sharply. They slow down and grow higher until they crash onto the shore.

Wave power

Tsunamis caused by earthquakes and volcanoes—tectonic tsunamis—are powerful enough to reshape coastlines and can travel thousands of miles across oceans. Local tsunamis, caused by landslides, can cause higher waves than tectonic tsunamis, but these do not usually travel very far. When earthquakes generate both tectonic and local tsunamis, the effect can be devastating. The biggest tsunamis of all are caused by asteroid impacts. But it is not just the origin of the tsunami that affects its power. If a tsunami invades a bay, the shape of the coastline can channel the waves, making them narrower, higher, and more destructive.

WAVE OR TSUNAMI
Ordinary wind-generated waves like this one roll in to break on the shore about every 10 seconds, with about 500 ft (150 m) between the crest of each wave. When a tsunami hits the shore, it rarely forms a breaker like this. There can be a much as 300 miles (500 km) between the crest of each wave, and there may be more than an hour between the arrival of each wave.

HARBOR WAVE
On November 18, 1867, the steamship *La Plata* was struck by a tsunami that hit the island of St. Thomas, in the Virgin Islands. An earthquake measuring 7.5 on the Richter scale had sent a tsunami racing toward the coast. Eyewitnesses described a wall of water 20 ft (6.1 m) high sweeping over the island's harbor.

A breaking wave can generate a force equivalent to the thrust of a space rocket's main engines

Rock face stripped of vegetation by the tsunami is still bare 14 years later

THE BIGGEST TSUNAMI
On July 9, 1958, an earthquake measuring 8.3 sent 100 million tons of rock crashing into Lituya Bay, Alaska. A giant splash surged to a height of 1,720 ft (525 m), stripping away the vegetation to leave bare rock. A rock slide then created a local tsunami over 100 ft (30 m) high—the largest tsunami in recent history. It swept across the bay, flooding inland and uprooting thousands of trees.

SEA SCULPTURE
The extraordinary towers and caves of Cathedral Rocks, New South Wales, Australia, were cut away from the cliffs and gouged out in just a few minutes by the power of a tsunami thousands of years ago. According to scientists, the rocks must have been sculpted by the most powerful types of tsunami—caused by a huge asteroid hitting the ocean or a massive landslide on the seabed.

Oil-carrying truck hurled about by tsunami

BURNING WATERS
On Good Friday in March 1964, an earthquake off the Alaska coast caused landslides which created a 30 ft (9 m) local tsunami in the town of Seward. Oil-storage tanks along the bay were damaged and their fuel ignited. Twenty minutes later, the first 40 ft (12 m) wave of a tectonic tsunami washed in, spreading a wall of flaming oil into Seward and setting most of the town on fire.

TSUNAMIS AND TIDAL BORES
When a tsunami-generated wave reaches a river mouth or a bay, the shape of the land on either side funnels the wave into a narrow, high wall of seawater weighing billions of tons. Exceptionally high tides create similar walls of water called bores. Here, a tidal bore sweeps over the embankment of the Qiantang River in eastern China, surprising tourists. Bores along the Qiantang River have been as high as 30 ft (9 m), moving at 25 mph (40 kph).

Walls of water

THE EARTHQUAKE that triggered the Indian Ocean tsunami of December 26, 2004, unleashed energy equivalent to the detonation of thousands of nuclear weapons. Ocean waves radiated out from the undersea earthquake close to the island of Sumatra in Indonesia. The strongest traveled east and west. Bangladesh, to the north of the epicenter, had few casualties, while Somalia, far away to the west on the coast of Africa, was hit much harder. But the pounding waves did not hit only those coasts in a direct line from the epicenter. Some waves were bent around land masses to hit coasts away from the epicenter, such as the western coasts of Sri Lanka and India.

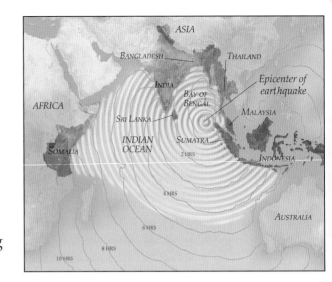

TSUNAMI TRAVEL TIME
Shock waves spread out from the epicenter of the earthquake like the ripples when a stone is dropped into water. Each pink line on the map indicates one hour of travel time. The waves took just 15 minutes to reach the nearest land, Sumatra. Seven hours later, the coast of Somalia was struck. The effects of the tsunami even caused minor damage as far away as northern Australia.

SEISMOGRAM
This seismograph reading shows the earthquake that shook southern Asia just before 8 a.m., local time. Most earthquakes, even major ones, last only a few seconds. These tremors went on for nearly 10 minutes. When they subsided, no one realized that the earthquake had triggered something even more deadly—a tsunami.

Before a tsunami, the sea can recede by as much as 1.6 miles (2.5 km) on gently sloping shores

THE CALM BEFORE THE STORM
Up to half an hour before the tsunami struck, the ocean suddenly appeared to drain away from some beaches. When the trough—the low part of a wave—reaches the shore before the peak, it sucks the water offshore. This is called drawback and is an urgent warning to leave the beach. However, many people around the Indian Ocean went to investigate the exposed sand, with tragic results.

TIDE FLOODING SRI LANKA
This photograph, taken from a hotel room looking down on a beach-side resort in southwest Sri Lanka, shows the moment the massive wave struck, two hours after the earthquake. Waves up to 30 ft (10 m) high rushed in like a very strong, very fast tide, and kept coming, sweeping in between the buildings and trees.

BANDA ACEH
The place most devastated by the tsunami's onslaught was the Indonesian city of Banda Aceh, on the island of Sumatra. The city was just 155 miles (250 km) from the earthquake's epicenter and, when the waves receded, it lay in ruins. Many eyewitnesses compared the ravaged city to Hiroshima in Japan, after the detonation of an atomic bomb in 1945. One hundred thousand people may have lost their lives in the Banda province in just 15 minutes.

Buildings utterly flattened

WRECKED BOATS, INDIA
Not only were lives lost in the tsunami, but livelihoods, too. All around the Indian Ocean, fishing boats lay in heaps on the shore, many battered beyond repair, like these in the south Indian state of Tamil Nadu. The tsunami destroyed two-thirds of Tamil Nadu's fishing fleet.

TWISTED TRACK
Near Seenigama, on the southwestern coast of Sri Lanka, 1,500 passengers perished when the full force of the tsunami hit the train they were traveling on. The waves not only swept the engine and cars from the track, but forced up the rails themselves, leaving a mass of twisted wood, metal, and tangled debris.

Japanese tsunami

THE TSUNAMI THAT STRUCK JAPAN on March 11, 2011, was one of the most catastrophic ever recorded. Huge waves sweeping in from the ocean reached record heights of up to 133 ft (40.5 m) above normal sea level, destroying virtually everything in their path. Thousands died as the debris-loaded water surged inland, flattening coastal cities and cutting road and rail links. The floodwater also wrecked a nuclear power plant, releasing radiation that could take decades to clean up.

EARTH SHOCK
The tsunami was caused by a colossal earthquake on the ocean floor 43 miles (70 km) off Honshu, the main Japanese island. This building, in Onagawa in the Miyagi prefecture, was destroyed by the earthquake and tsunami. The earthquake was the biggest ever recorded in Japan, but its destructive power was dwarfed by that of the tsunami it unleashed.

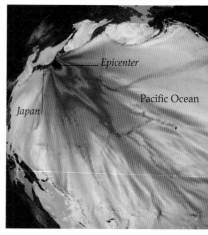

RADIATING WAVES
On the ocean floor off Japan, one section of Earth's crust is pushing beneath another, bending it downward. In March 2011, the boundary between the two gave way and the section nearest Japan sprang back up, raising the seabed by up to 23 ft (7 m). This pushed up huge waves that traveled all across the Pacific, as this map shows, with the darker colors, such as black indicating highest waves, and red and orange indicating relatively smaller waves.

SURGING WATER
When the tsunami waves reached shallow coastal water, they slowed down and built up, rising far higher than anyone had thought possible. Sea defenses that had been built to resist tsunamis were completely overwhelmed, as seen here at the northern fishing port of Miyako. Here, the sea rose to at least 28 ft (8.5 m) above normal high tide level. Cars parked on the ocean side of the sea wall were lifted up and over by surging water, along with fishing boats that were ripped from their moorings.

NUCLEAR CRISIS

At the Fukushima nuclear power plant on the eastern coast of Japan, the nuclear reactors shut down automatically after the initial earthquake. They were still generating heat, but this was carried away by a cooling system powered by emergency pumps. When the plant was hit by the tsunami 50 minutes later, the wave swept right over its 19 ft- (5.8 m-) sea wall. It flooded the site, knocking out the emergency pumps. This led the reactors to overheat with disastrous results.

DESPERATE RESCUE

When the giant waves finally stopped sweeping in from the ocean, survivors and rescue workers combed through the wreckage looking for trapped victims. This young girl was rescued from the shattered ruins of Kesennuma, a fishing port lying to the north of the earthquake epicenter. The port was hit by a deadly combination of the earthquake, tsunami, and raging fires.

MELTDOWN

As the crippled nuclear reactors at Fukushima got hotter, the radioactive fuel rods that generate the heat started to melt. Eventually, three of the six reactors suffered full meltdown, creating pools of radioactive molten metal. This situation was made worse when three reactor buildings were wrecked by explosions, seen here from the air. Meanwhile, stored fuel rods in nearby water tanks also overheated, threatening to release more radioactivity. Everyone living within 19 miles (30 km) of the plant had to be evacuated.

Debris piled up by the tsunami waves

INNOCENT VICTIMS

More than 18,000 people were killed by the earthquake and tsunami—90 percent of them drowned by the raging floodwaters. Many more were left homeless, including at least 100,000 children. Here, a salvaged blanket offers scant comfort to a shocked survivor gazing at the destruction in Ishinomaki, where one school lost 74 of its 108 students to the disaster.

Recovery begins

As THE SCALE of any tsunami disaster becomes apparent, aid starts to arrive from around the globe. The first task is to provide shelter and medical assistance to survivors.Then, locals and aid workers must clear the debris left by the water. One of the most traumatic jobs is clearing away the bodies of the victims before they start to rot and spread disease. Once the clearing operations are over, people can begin to get back to their regular lives, going to school and work. But recovery can take a long time, especially if the tsunami destroys vital infrastructure, such as power plants, and the shock and grief suffered by its victims may take even longer to heal.

IN MEMORY OF THE DEAD
This Buddhist statue was left on the beach at Khao Lak, Thailand, in memory of those who died in the 2004 Asian tsunami. Religious services for the victims were held all around the coast.

Refugee camp at Bang Muang, Phang Tha, in Thailand

HEALTH CHECK
Medical personnel check a child for radiation exposure in Fukushima city, Japan, after the 2011 tsunami disaster caused catastrophic damage to the Fukushima nuclear power plant. As the nuclear reactors overheated and started leaking radioactive material, radiation levels rose well above safe limits. The whole area was evacuated, but the health of the local people will have to be closely monitored for many years to come.

Elephant handler wears mask as protection against the smell of decaying bodies

TENT CITY
Vast camps were set up to house people made homeless by the 2004 Asian tsunami. Many feared that poor sanitation in the huge refugee camps might lead to outbreaks of diseases such as cholera and typhoid. This was prevented by the swift action of local and national health services. Their first priority was that survivors had safe drinking water and food, the means to cook, essentials such as soap, and adequate sanitation.

ELEPHANTS AT WORK
After the 2004 Asian disaster, it was essential to bury corpses quickly to prevent outbreaks of disease. Thailand's elephants, usually employed in the logging or tourist industries, proved invaluable now. Elephants could reach areas inaccessible even to four-wheel-drive trucks. First, dogs were used to sniff out bodies, then the elephants could nudge aside lumber, masonry, or fallen trees to reveal the corpses hidden beneath. They also carried out the grim task of transporting the bodies to burial sites.

CLEARING THE DAMAGE
Rescue personnel search for missing residents in Miyagi prefecture on March 15, 2011, following the massive earthquake and tsunami on March 11. Japan's government urged people against panic-buying of food and supplies, as the country grappled with the aftermath, including the resulting nuclear crisis.

BOAT BUILDING
On Asian coasts hit by the tsunami of 2004, local people set to work to rebuild boats that had been damaged or destroyed by the waves. Boats are vital to the region's fishing industry, but many tourist resorts also use them to show visitors the region's coral reefs and rich marine life.

Temporary shelter for aid workers and their equipment

Boat building on the beach at Phuket, Thailand

BACK TO SCHOOL
Schoolchildren starting the new school year after the 2011 Japanese tsunami had to come to terms with terrible losses. These children at an elementary school in Natori, northern Japan, lost many of their friends when the school was flooded. Many were also made homeless when their houses were swept away.

Tsunami warnings

Tsunami evacuation sign

IN 2004 THE ASIAN TSUNAMI struck the Indian Ocean out of the blue, taking most of its victims by surprise. In the Pacific, there was a tsunami warning system. Oceanographers were employed to monitor the ocean for possible tsunamis, analysing data from earthquake and ocean-wave sensors and using sirens and broadcasts to warn people on vulnerable shores. In 2006, a similar scheme was set up in the Indian Ocean, but all such systems have their limitations. The earthquake that triggered the 2011 Japanese tsunami was so close to Japan that the tsunami struck just 50 minutes later—so even though a tsunami warning was issued, people living on the coast had little time to escape.

TSUNAMI OBSERVATION
A sensor attached to the ocean floor below this Japanese buoy measures the pressure of water above it. If a tsunami as small as ½ in (1 cm) passes over it, the water pressure changes and the sensor sends a signal to the buoy on the sea surface. The buoy then signals a satellite, which alerts Japan's Tsunami Early Warning Center.

Antenna for sending signals to satellite

Solar panels power the buoy

Gate raised to allow tall ships into the harbor

Gate of 920 tons (840 metric tons)

HOLDING BACK THE WAVES
This enormous floodgate in Nomazu Port, Japan, has a door 30 ft (9.3 m) high, which automatically shuts against tsunamis. It is triggered by a seismograph—an earthquake-measuring device—which senses the Earth movements that could lead to a tsunami. Most of Japan's population live along the coast, so measures like this are vital to protect the crowded cities of this earthquake-prone region.

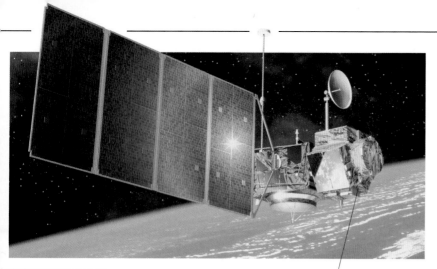

THE SEA FROM SPACE
Launched in 1992, the Poseidon satellite records the ocean currents and sea surface height from its orbit above Earth. Tiny fluctuations in sea level immediately after an undersea earthquake can give advance warning of a tsunami.

Two radar altimeters measure sea surface height

TSUNAMI WARNING TOWER
When the Warning Center spots an impending tsunami, the race is on to spread the news around coasts that may be affected. New warning towers, like this one in Thailand, are being built all around the Indian Ocean. The tower has a siren, and its antennae can interrupt TV and radio broadcasts to send text messages to warn the public that they should move to higher ground, away from the coast.

TSUNAMI WARNING CENTER
Oceanographers at the Pacific Tsunami Warning Center in Hawaii gather information about undersea earthquakes and sea level fluctuations to determine whether a tsunami is likely. Within half an hour of an earthquake, they can send out warnings, predicting where and when the tsunami will arrive. A similar warning system is being put in place around the Indian Ocean.

SONAR DEVICE
The first step in establishing an Indian Ocean tsunami warning system is to begin monitoring earthquake activity on the seabed in the region. This sonar device is being launched to map the seabed near Banda Aceh, where the 2004 tsunami originated. It will reflect sound off the seabed and build up a 3-D image.

Tourists relax in front of the Tsunami Warning Tower at Phuket, Thailand

Land areas above sea level

Steep slope leading to ocean depths

Areas below sea level are blue/green

THE OCEAN FLOOR IN 3-D
This false-colored 3-D image of the ocean floor around California was made using sonar. Sonar maps like this enable oceanographers to study the contours of the seabed. Regular scanning reveals seabed movement, which could signal tsunami-triggering events. Such movement includes shifts along a fault line, or the collapse of unstable undersea slopes at the edges of continents.

Mighty volcanoes

Underneath the earth's solid crust lie pockets of burning hot molten rock called magma. Less dense than the rock above it, magma rises to the surface through weak spots in the crust. Most of these weaknesses lie along the margins of the Earth's tectonic plates, but a few are found at hotspots (areas of deep heat within the Earth) far from the plate edges, such as the Hawaiian islands and Yellowstone in Wyoming. As the magma pushes upward, pressure builds until the magma breaks through the Earth's crust, sending rock, ash, and lava cascading or oozing onto the surface as a volcano.

GODDESS PELE
According to legend, the Hawaiian goddess of volcanoes, Pele, has all the powers of a volcano. She is said to make mountains, melt rocks, destroy forests, and build new islands.

SLEEPING VOLCANO
Japan's beautiful Mount Fuji last erupted in 1707 and is now classed as dormant. Dormant volcanoes show no signs of activity, but they may erupt in the future. Active volcanoes erupt constantly, or with gaps of a few years. Volcanoes that have been dormant for thousands of years are called extinct—although scientists cannot be certain that they will never erupt again.

Ashy steam blasting from the volcano's vent

FIERY RIVER
When the magma inside a volcano is runny and does not contain much gas, it oozes or gushes from the volcano in a hot stream of lava, like this pahoehoe (pah-hoy-hoy) lava in Hawaii. When the magma is thick and sticky, it traps gases such as steam and carbon dioxide inside it. Sticky, viscous magma erupts from the volcano in a violent explosion of lava globules and burning ash.

Molten lava sets fire to trees

Cracks and ridges form as the top of the lava sheet hardens

BIRTH OF AN ISLAND
The majority of volcanic eruptions take place under the oceans. In 1963, an undersea eruption occurred off the coast of Iceland with unusual results. The sea began to steam as seawater poured into the volcano's vent and was boiled by its heat. Over the next three and a half years, lava and ash from the volcano piled up, eventually forming an entirely new island, Surtsey, measuring 1 sq mile (2.5 sq km) in area.

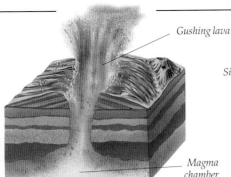

Gushing lava

Magma chamber

SHIELD CONE VOLCANO
Runny lava escapes from the volcano's vent (opening) in a fountain or a gushing river. This type of lava runs easily along the ground, spreading over a wide area. Successive eruptions form a massive mountain with gently sloping sides. A typical shield cone volcano is Mauna Kea, Hawaii.

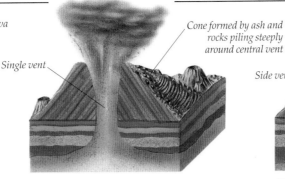

Single vent

Cone formed by ash and rocks piling steeply around central vent

CINDER CONE VOLCANO
Erupts ash and rocky material, which falls in a ring. These volcanoes usually have only one vent. The straight-sided, cone-shaped crater is created by the rocks and rock fragments from many eruptions. Cinder cones, such as Paricutin, Mexico, rarely rise more than 1,000 ft (300 m) above land.

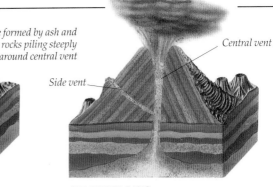

Central vent

Side vent

STRATOVOLCANO
The lava is thick and sticky, so it cools and hardens quickly, producing a steep, symmetrical mountain. Eruptions of lava alternate with rocky and ashy material, producing distinct layers in the mountain. Stratovolcanoes may grow more than 10,000 ft (3,050 m) high, and can be cone- or dome-shaped.

TAKING THE TEMPERATURE
Volcanologists (scientists who study volcanoes) can find out what is going on beneath the Earth's surface by measuring the ground temperature around volcanic vents. Active volcanoes have to be monitored frequently, so that people can be warned when an eruption is likely. If the ground temperature rises, it may be a warning of an impending eruption.

TAKING SAMPLES
After eruptions, volcanologists dressed in heat-protective suits collect fresh lava samples for analysis. They have to work fast, since further eruptions are always possible. Lava samples can provide information about changes in a volcano's behavior. For example, scientists may analyze the mixture of gases in the lava to see if they have become more explosive.

Rivers of fire

THE DEVASTATING POWER of an exploding volcano is a magnificent and terrifying sight. As the volcanic cone becomes unplugged, enormous pressures are released, forcing lava, ash, rocks, and superheated gases out. After an eruption, people may return to farm the soil nearby, particularly if it is now nourished with mineral-rich volcanic ash. Fortunately, today most eruptions can be predicted and people can be evacuated from the danger zone. However, the effects of a volcanic eruption can reach far wider than the foot of the mountain. A major eruption can affect the weather over the whole world.

JETS OF FIRE
In 2001, Italy's Mount Etna exploded with a bang. Rising 11,120 ft (3,390 m) above the island of Sicily, Etna is one of Europe's highest mountains, and its most active volcano. Usually, it erupts in small, continuous bursts like a firework display. Local people fight a constant battle with lava flows that damage roads, buildings, farmland, and threaten towns. Concrete barriers, trenches, even explosives have been used in attempts to redirect the lava but with limited success.

Plume of volcanic ash

MOUNT ST. HELENS
When Mount St. Helens in Washington erupted on May 18, 1980, a column of gas, ash, and pumice was sent hurtling 15 miles (24 km) up into the atmosphere. So much rock was blown off the top of the mountain that it lost 1,350 ft (400 m) in height. A cloud of ash spread over an area of 20,000 sq miles (50,000 sq km), causing a major hazard for aircraft.

Uprooted and burned fir trees

AFTER THE ERUPTION
The Mount St. Helens eruption flattened around 230 sq miles (600 sq km) of forest, and wiped out virtually all the local wildlife. Scientists estimate that it will take 200 years for the forest to return to its pre-eruption condition.

Fern

Lichen

Moss

NEW LIFE
After a volcanic eruption, the first plants to appear in solidified lava are mosses, lichens, and small weeds. It may take decades for the volcanic rock to break down into fertile soil. Once this happens, larger plants begin to take root.

PYROCLASTIC FLOW
After lying dormant for 600 years, on June 15, 1991, Mount Pinatubo in the Philippines began erupting. A gigantic column of rock particles and ash was ejected 25 miles (40 km) into the atmosphere. As the column collapsed, this deadly cloud of hot gas and debris, called a pyroclastic flow, hurtled at speeds of 100 mph (160 kph) across the surrounding area. Haze spread across the globe.

DEADLY DUST
As ash from Mount Pinatubo filled the air with a choking cloud and covered the fields, farmers took their buffalo to look for unaffected areas. Many survivors developed pneumonia from inhaling the gritty ash, and entire harvests were lost.

PANIC IN POMPEII
The prosperous Roman town of Pompeii lay in the shadow of Italy's Mount Vesuvius. The volcano had been dormant for centuries, so the townspeople were taken by surprise when they felt the first rumbles of an eruption on August 24, 79 CE. This artist's impression shows the pyroclastic flow about to engulf the town.

Ash around the bodies hardened, preserving the shapes of the dead

Fluid lava pours down the slopes

DEADLY DUST
Many people managed to escape from Pompeii, but some 2,000 were trapped in the town. They died of suffocation as a choking pyroclastic flow swept through the streets. Pompeii and its dead were buried under 100 ft (30 m) of ash, and not discovered until excavations began in 1860.

Landslides and avalanches

ONE TYPE OF NATURAL DISASTER can happen in any part of the world. Wherever a steep hillside is found, when the pull of gravity is greater than the forces that hold together the particles on the slope, a mass of loose material may come crashing down the slope. On a rocky or muddy hillside, unstable rocks and soil can cause a landslide. On a snowy mountainside, snow can hurtle as an avalanche, burying people and buildings in its path. Speedy rescue is essential to save any survivors buried under the dense snow or masses of rocks and mud. For hundreds of years, rescue teams have used dogs to find trapped people.

St. Bernard rescue dog

AVALANCHE WARNING SIGN
In mountain ski resorts, such as the Swiss Alps and the Rockies in the US and Canada, warning signs indicate the risk of avalanches. Although it is difficult to predict exactly when and where an avalanche will take place, experts can tell when the snow layers begin to become unstable enough to trigger an avalanche.

TO THE RESCUE
High in the mountains, rescue teams use helicopters to reach injured people quickly. A winch is used to lower rescuers and haul up the injured on stretchers. The pilot must be careful, since even the noise and draft of a helicopter can trigger another avalanche.

TORRENT OF SNOW
An avalanche starts when mountain snow builds into an unstable overhang or becomes loose because of a thaw. Triggered by a ground tremor or by a loud noise, the avalanche grows as it rolls down the slope, loosening more snow and picking up rocks and soil. The path of an avalanche can be ½ mile (800 m) wide. Anyone caught up in it has just a five percent chance of survival.

AVALANCHE PREVENTION
Fences built across the slopes can bring tumbling snow to a halt before it has a chance to grow into a huge avalanche. Sometimes, explosives are used to trigger small, controlled avalanches. This prevents the build-up of large snow masses that could cause a major avalanche.

TYPES OF LANDSLIDE

There are four types of landslide. Soil creep is a slow movement—as its name suggests—due to tiny shifts in the soil particles. Slumping is a faster slide, occurring when slabs of land slip down a slope. Debris flow happens when a slope becomes saturated with water and triggers a landslide of a water-soaked mass of soil and rocks. Rockfalls are sudden slides caused by heavy rain or frost dislodging larger rock pieces.

Steep, water-saturated slope

Loose pieces of rock

Rockfall

Debris flow

Slumping

Soil creep

ROCKY ROAD

In August 1983, a 20 ft- (6 m-) slab of granite crashed down from the hillside onto the highway in Yosemite National Park, California. Rockfalls along roads are often the result of poor construction methods. Road-builders may cut into hillsides without supporting them properly or build on slopes that are too steep.

SLIPPING INTO THE SEA

The coast can be a dangerous place to build. In 1993, the clay slope beneath this hotel in Scarborough, UK, became saturated with water and slumped into the sea, taking part of the building with it. Even solid stone cliffs can be eroded by wind-driven rain and waves until the cliff top is left overhanging precariously.

Part of hotel reduced to landslide rubble

Rescue workers carry the body of a landslide victim

DEADLY DEBRIS

An earthquake measuring 7.6 on the Richter scale hit San Salvador, El Salvador, on January, 13, 2001. It triggered a massive debris flow in the Santa Tecla neighborhood. Soil and rocks swept down the hillside, cutting straight through the streets and homes below. Buildings directly in the path of the debris flow were flattened, killing 63 people.

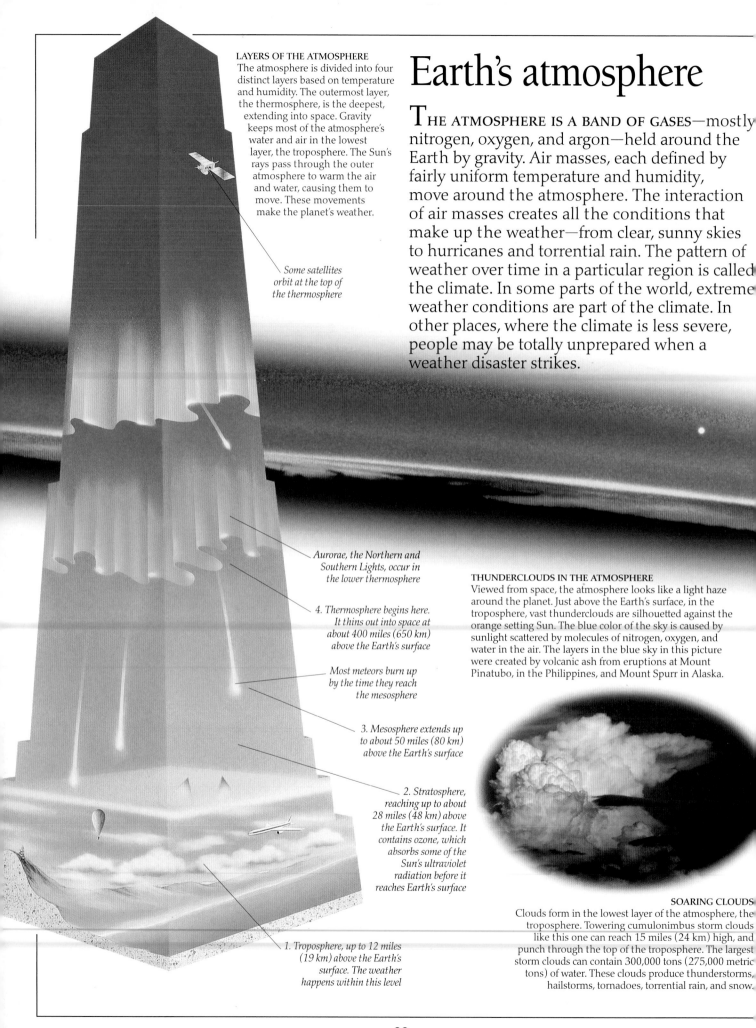

LAYERS OF THE ATMOSPHERE
The atmosphere is divided into four distinct layers based on temperature and humidity. The outermost layer, the thermosphere, is the deepest, extending into space. Gravity keeps most of the atmosphere's water and air in the lowest layer, the troposphere. The Sun's rays pass through the outer atmosphere to warm the air and water, causing them to move. These movements make the planet's weather.

Some satellites orbit at the top of the thermosphere

Earth's atmosphere

THE ATMOSPHERE IS A BAND OF GASES—mostly nitrogen, oxygen, and argon—held around the Earth by gravity. Air masses, each defined by fairly uniform temperature and humidity, move around the atmosphere. The interaction of air masses creates all the conditions that make up the weather—from clear, sunny skies to hurricanes and torrential rain. The pattern of weather over time in a particular region is called the climate. In some parts of the world, extreme weather conditions are part of the climate. In other places, where the climate is less severe, people may be totally unprepared when a weather disaster strikes.

Aurorae, the Northern and Southern Lights, occur in the lower thermosphere

4. Thermosphere begins here. It thins out into space at about 400 miles (650 km) above the Earth's surface

Most meteors burn up by the time they reach the mesosphere

3. Mesosphere extends up to about 50 miles (80 km) above the Earth's surface

2. Stratosphere, reaching up to about 28 miles (48 km) above the Earth's surface. It contains ozone, which absorbs some of the Sun's ultraviolet radiation before it reaches Earth's surface

1. Troposphere, up to 12 miles (19 km) above the Earth's surface. The weather happens within this level

THUNDERCLOUDS IN THE ATMOSPHERE
Viewed from space, the atmosphere looks like a light haze around the planet. Just above the Earth's surface, in the troposphere, vast thunderclouds are silhouetted against the orange setting Sun. The blue color of the sky is caused by sunlight scattered by molecules of nitrogen, oxygen, and water in the air. The layers in the blue sky in this picture were created by volcanic ash from eruptions at Mount Pinatubo, in the Philippines, and Mount Spurr in Alaska.

SOARING CLOUDS
Clouds form in the lowest layer of the atmosphere, the troposphere. Towering cumulonimbus storm clouds like this one can reach 15 miles (24 km) high, and punch through the top of the troposphere. The largest storm clouds can contain 300,000 tons (275,000 metric tons) of water. These clouds produce thunderstorms, hailstorms, tornadoes, torrential rain, and snow.

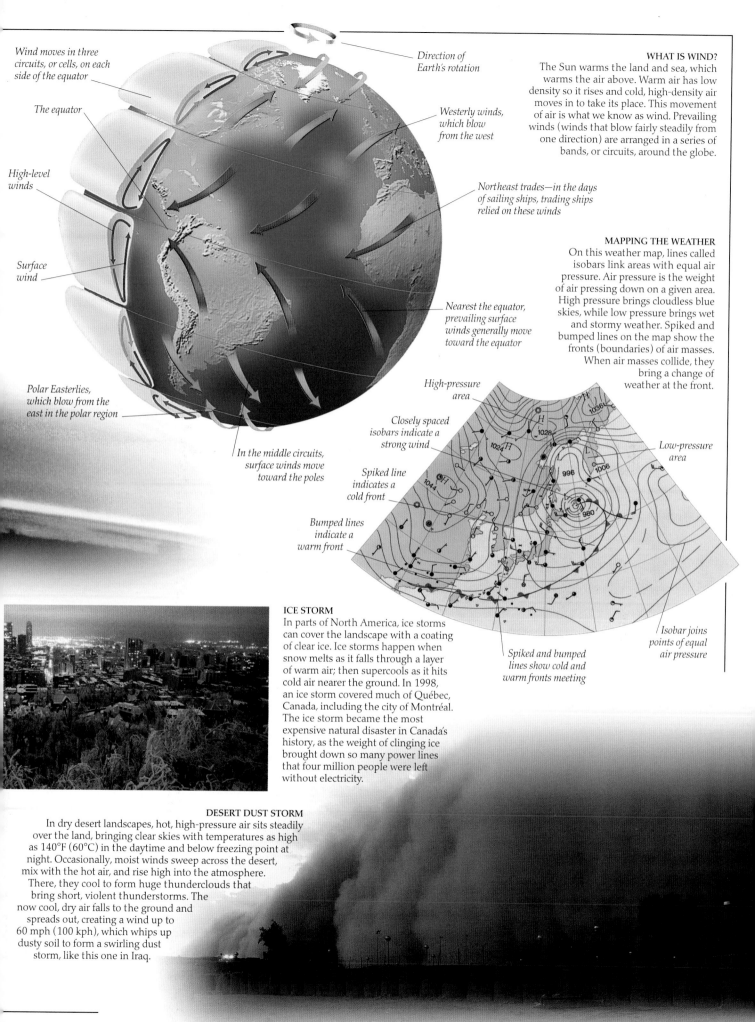

Wind moves in three circuits, or cells, on each side of the equator

The equator

High-level winds

Surface wind

Polar Easterlies, which blow from the east in the polar region

In the middle circuits, surface winds move toward the poles

Direction of Earth's rotation

Westerly winds, which blow from the west

Northeast trades—in the days of sailing ships, trading ships relied on these winds

Nearest the equator, prevailing surface winds generally move toward the equator

WHAT IS WIND?

The Sun warms the land and sea, which warms the air above. Warm air has low density so it rises and cold, high-density air moves in to take its place. This movement of air is what we know as wind. Prevailing winds (winds that blow fairly steadily from one direction) are arranged in a series of bands, or circuits, around the globe.

MAPPING THE WEATHER

On this weather map, lines called isobars link areas with equal air pressure. Air pressure is the weight of air pressing down on a given area. High pressure brings cloudless blue skies, while low pressure brings wet and stormy weather. Spiked and bumped lines on the map show the fronts (boundaries) of air masses. When air masses collide, they bring a change of weather at the front.

High-pressure area

Closely spaced isobars indicate a strong wind

Spiked line indicates a cold front

Bumped lines indicate a warm front

Low-pressure area

Spiked and bumped lines show cold and warm fronts meeting

Isobar joins points of equal air pressure

ICE STORM

In parts of North America, ice storms can cover the landscape with a coating of clear ice. Ice storms happen when snow melts as it falls through a layer of warm air; then supercools as it hits cold air nearer the ground. In 1998, an ice storm covered much of Québec, Canada, including the city of Montréal. The ice storm became the most expensive natural disaster in Canada's history, as the weight of clinging ice brought down so many power lines that four million people were left without electricity.

DESERT DUST STORM

In dry desert landscapes, hot, high-pressure air sits steadily over the land, bringing clear skies with temperatures as high as 140°F (60°C) in the daytime and below freezing point at night. Occasionally, moist winds sweep across the desert, mix with the hot air, and rise high into the atmosphere. There, they cool to form huge thunderclouds that bring short, violent thunderstorms. The now cool, dry air falls to the ground and spreads out, creating a wind up to 60 mph (100 kph), which whips up dusty soil to form a swirling dust storm, like this one in Iraq.

Wild weather

Aт any time, across the world, about 2,000 thunderstorms are lighting up the sky with giant electrical sparks. A bolt of lightning can reach 54,000°F (30,000°C), five times hotter than the surface of the Sun. The massive electrical charge that a lightning bolt carries can kill in an instant. Most thunderstorms happen in summer, when warm air rises to form thunderclouds. These storms can bring torrential rain or stinging hail. Meteorologists track the path of thunderstorms, using information from satellites, weather stations on the ground, and specially adapted weather planes that can fly into storms.

EIFFEL TOWER STRUCK
This dramatic photograph shows lightning striking the Eiffel Tower in Paris, France. Like other tall buildings, the Eiffel Tower is protected from such damage by a lightning rod—a metal cable or strap that leads the electrical charge down to the ground where it discharges harmlessly.

THUNDER AND LIGHTNING
Inside a storm cloud, water droplets and ice crystals rise and fall violently, building up a massive static electrical charge. The charge sends a spark of lightning to the ground, creating fork lightning, or among the clouds, making sheet lightning. The air around the lightning heats up instantly and expands, creating a shock wave that is heard as a clap of thunder.

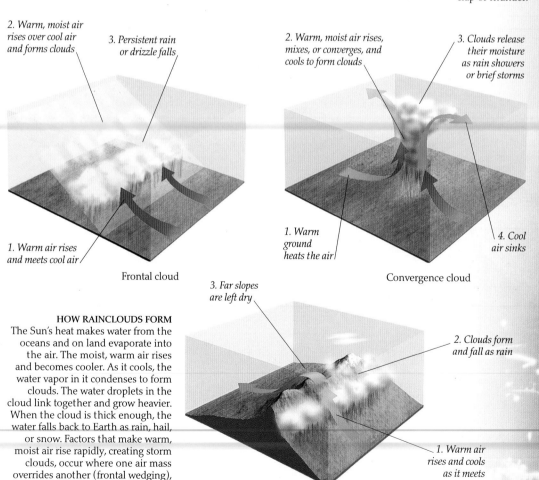

2. Warm, moist air rises over cool air and forms clouds

3. Persistent rain or drizzle falls

1. Warm air rises and meets cool air

Frontal cloud

2. Warm, moist air rises, mixes, or converges, and cools to form clouds

3. Clouds release their moisture as rain showers or brief storms

1. Warm ground heats the air

4. Cool air sinks

Convergence cloud

3. Far slopes are left dry

2. Clouds form and fall as rain

1. Warm air rises and cools as it meets the mountain

Mountain lifting

HOW RAINCLOUDS FORM
The Sun's heat makes water from the oceans and on land evaporate into the air. The moist, warm air rises and becomes cooler. As it cools, the water vapor in it condenses to form clouds. The water droplets in the cloud link together and grow heavier. When the cloud is thick enough, the water falls back to Earth as rain, hail, or snow. Factors that make warm, moist air rise rapidly, creating storm clouds, occur where one air mass overrides another (frontal wedging), where air converges, and where mountains uplift moving air.

FLYING INTO THE STORM
Airplanes such as this WC-130 Hercules are used to monitor weather in the US. Similar planes are used around the world. When severe weather is expected, such planes can fly into the storm to analyze the speed, strength, and direction of the wind. Meteorologists use this information to predict which areas will be struck by the storm and how badly.

Radar equipment in nose of plane

Tubes show the branching path of the lightning

LIGHTNING SCULPTURE
This weird sculpture of solidified sand was created by lightning. As lightning passes through sand, it heats up the sand grains to melting point and then fuses them together to form a structure of hollow tubes, called a fulgurite. Lightning's intense heat can ignite trees and wooden buildings, causing natural fires.

Thunderclouds over Gillette, Wyoming

BLACK CLOUDS AND HAIL
Hailstones form when raindrops, moving up and down in the freezing air inside black thunderclouds, become coated with layers of ice. Large hailstones can be bigger than a baseball, but most are the size of a pea. Even when they are tiny, these balls of ice can cause havoc, battering fields of crops, damaging property, and turning roads into hazardous, slippery ice rinks.

Giant hailstone

Baseball

Hurricane force

Storm at sea

IN LATE SUMMER, above the warm, tropical seas that lie on each side of the equator, enormous rotating storm systems can develop with wind speeds of 75 mph (120 kph) and above. These storms are called hurricanes when they originate over the Atlantic Ocean, cyclones in the Indian Ocean, and typhoons in the Pacific. The biggest measure 300–500 miles (500–800 km) across. These storms can travel thousands of miles, sweeping inland from the ocean, and leave a trail of destruction. High winds toss boats around, uproot trees, and topple buildings, while torrential rain and surges of seawater bring devastating floods.

DARK THREAT
Tropical storms are fueled by the heat of the Sun evaporating water from the ocean. The water vapor is carried upward by the rising warm air, building colossal storm clouds. As the weight of air is lifted, a zone of very low atmospheric pressure is created. The surrounding air then rushes into the low-pressure zone, driving the howling winds of a hurricane.

HURRICANE FORMING
This satellite image shows spiral bands of cloud forming Hurricane Ivan, as it passes over the Cayman Islands in the Atlantic Ocean in September 2004. For a hurricane to form, the temperature of the sea must be above 80°F (27°C), fueling wind speeds greater than 74 mph (118 kph). A hurricane can pick up two billion tons of water vapor from the sea each day, to be dumped on land as torrential rain.

Blue arrows show cool air spiraling outward at top of hurricane

Dry air sinks into the eye of the storm

Eye area

Air spirals inward at bottom of hurricane

The fastest winds and heaviest rain spiral around the low-pressure eye wall

Sea surface bulges in the low-pressure eye area

Red arrows show spiraling bands of wind and rain

INSIDE A HURRICANE
A hurricane is created by an area of warm air rising above the ocean, and sucking in surrounding air. The Earth's rotation makes the air spin. As the spinning air rises, it cools, creating a spiral of towering storm clouds. At the center of the hurricane is an area of calm air known as the eye.

The calm eye of the storm

Thick clouds spiral around the eye

EL NIÑO

Every three to seven years, a weather pattern called El Niño causes winds over the Pacific to change direction temporarily. This colored satellite image shows the difference between the normal sea temperatures worldwide and those that occurred during the 1997 El Niño event. The winds push warm water toward South America, bringing hurricanes and other tropical storms, while countries to the west of the ocean may experience drought.

Red shows sea temperatures farthest above normal

Purple shows sea temperatures farthest below normal

EYE OF THE STORM

Hurricane Fran's fiercest wind and most torrential rain batter a gas station in North Carolina in 1996. The most violent part of the hurricane often follows a calm period, when it might seem that the storm has passed. In the midst of the whirling wind and rain, the sky may suddenly clear and the air grow still, as the eye of the storm passes. A few moments later, the storm returns with renewed vigor.

HURRICANE WARNINGS

Flags such as these alert residents and ships when a hurricane is approaching the coast. Weather forecasters also broadcast an advance warning called a weather watch on television, radio, and the internet, telling people to look and listen for updates. Once the storm is certain to strike, a severe weather warning is broadcast. The best place to shelter is inside a brick or concrete building, far away from the windows.

WIND AND WAVES

In 1998, Hurricane Georges sent huge waves crashing onto the shore of Florida. When the eye passes over the coast, it brings with it a towering wall of water called a storm surge, which can reach 10 ft (3 m) high. This terrifying surge in sea level is caused by low air pressure at the storm's center, and it is responsible for many of the deaths that occur during hurricanes.

Palm trees bend but rarely break in hurricane winds

3. Andrew over the
Gulf of Mexico, August 25

1. Hurricane Andrew at
sea, August 23, 1992

2. Andrew passing over
Florida, August 24

Battling the wind

To PREDICT how a hurricane is
going to develop, meteorologists need
to measure its air pressure and wind
speed. Satellites can spot hurricanes
as they form, but the best way to
collect detailed, accurate pressure
and wind speed data is to send planes
known as Hurricane Hunters right
inside the hurricane. Even with all
this information, hurricane forecasting
can be tricky. When a hurricane moves
over land, it gradually runs out of
energy, but if it sweeps on out to sea,
warmth from the water can speed
up the wind once more. Every year,
around 90 hurricanes batter the
world's vulnerable coasts.

HURRICANE HUNTERS
During a 12-hour flight through
Hurricane Floyd in 1999, hurricane
hunters recorded wind speed,
humidity, and pressure in the heart
of the storm. The data was sent to a
weather station, where a computer
analyzed it to predict the path of
Floyd. Predictions give a general
guide, but hurricanes can change
direction unexpectedly.

*This infrared satellite image of
Hurricane Floyd helped the hurricane
hunters plan their flight path*

CAPSIZED YACHTS
One of the fiercest storms in US history,
Hurricane Andrew tore through Florida
in August 1992. A storm surge 17 ft
(5.2 m) high left yachts in Key Biscayne's
marina in a jumbled heap. The storm
weakened as it crossed Florida, but then
regained strength over the warm waters
of the Gulf of Mexico.

HURRICANE ANDREW
This sequence of satellite images shows the path of Hurricane Andrew as it traveled from east to west over three days in August 1992. Continuous wind speeds of 142 mph (228 kph) with gusts up to 200 mph (321 kph) were measured across Florida, before the force of the hurricane destroyed weather measuring devices. Andrew killed 26 people, although it narrowly missed the city of Miami, where many more lives could have been lost.

Wooden building, easily destroyed by a hurricane

THE GREAT STORM OF '87
In the middle of an October night in 1987, an unexpectedly severe storm hit southern Britain. As the storm brewed out in the Atlantic, it mixed with warm winds from the tail end of a hurricane. As a result, some of the wind gusts reached hurricane speeds of 122 mph (196 kph). The storm toppled 15 million trees and caused severe damage to buildings.

CYLONE NARGIS
The tropical cyclone that hit Myanmar on May 2, 2008, was the worst natural disaster in the country's recorded history. As the cyclone gathered strength in the Indian Ocean, it heaped up a 13-ft (4-m) storm surge—a giant wave that swept inland across the low-lying Irrawaddy Delta. The flooding caused catastrophic destruction, and killed at least 138,000.

Houseboat tipped over by massive waves

Trees uprooted by the force of the wind

PATH OF GEORGES, 1998
Holding on to each other to keep from being swept away by the 89-mph (144-kph) wind, these men struggled to reach the shelter of a solid building as Hurricane Georges tore across Florida. By the time the storm reached the US, it had already ravaged the Caribbean, taking more than 600 lives and ruining much of the region's crops.

Hurricane Katrina

WHEN HURRICANE KATRINA hit the southern US in August 2005, more than 1,000 people died in the most destructive and costly natural disaster in US history. In the aftermath of the storm, over a million people were left homeless and five million without power. The streets of the historic city of New Orleans lay under feet of water. Evacuees from the region were taken to makeshift emergency shelters in neighboring states or moved in with relatives and friends across the United States. Many said they were unlikely ever to return to the region where this catastrophic disaster had struck.

COURSE OF KATRINA
Hurricane Katrina passed over the Bahamas, south Florida, Louisiana, Mississippi, and Alabama between August 23 and 31, 2005. The wind reached a steady speed of 175 mph (280 kph) with even faster gusts. Katrina produced a storm surge that crashed onto a stretch of coastline over 200 miles (320 km) long. The wind finally began to lose strength and dropped below hurricane speed 150 miles (240 km) inland, near Jackson, Mississippi.

STORM SURGE
As the eye of the hurricane moved across the coast of Mississippi, it created a storm surge nearly 30 ft (10 m) high. In the town of Long Beach, cars and rubble were swept along by the surge, and dumped in a towering heap against the side of a building.

Sousaphone is too valuable to leave behind

LEAVING HOME
On August 28, with Hurricane Katrina heading for New Orleans, the city's mayor ordered everyone to evacuate. Five days after the storm, New Orleans was almost completely deserted. With electricity and water cut off and no food supplies, the last evacuees left their homes, clutching a few precious possessions.

UNDERWATER CITY
Rising floodwaters breached three of the levees—massive embankments—that were designed to protect New Orleans from flooding. By August 30, a day after Katrina hit the city, 80 percent of New Orleans was flooded. Some areas lay under 20 ft (6 m) of water. It took three weeks to repair the levees and pump the water out.

BROKEN WINDOWS
Curtains dangle outside hotel windows smashed by the force of Hurricane Katrina. Beds were seen flying out of the windows of one hotel. However, modern concrete and steel buildings like this one survived relatively unscathed. Many of New Orleans's famous wooden buildings, particularly those in the historic French Quarter, were completely destroyed. A commission was set up to advise the city government on how best to rebuild, taking into account the views and needs of all New Orleans' citizens.

BOAT RESCUE
Hundreds of thousands of New Orleans residents were left behind when the hurricane struck. Many of them gathered in evacuation centers to await rescue. After the storm, rescuers arrived in boats to pick up the people who were stranded and searched from house to house to check for other survivors.

Clear eye of the storm

Strong eyewall winds

A solitary car travels toward the city as most residents rush to leave

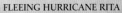

FLEEING HURRICANE RITA
Three weeks after Katrina, warnings of the arrival of Hurricane Rita sent residents of cities such as Houston, Texas, rushing to evacuate, fearing for their lives. Mass evacuations like this bring hazards of their own, since panicking drivers may cause accidents on the jammed roads. Fortunately, Hurricane Rita turned out to be much less severe than Katrina.

Twisting tornadoes

THE MOST VIOLENT WINDS on Earth, tornadoes (sometimes nicknamed twisters) can travel across the land at speeds of up to 125 mph (200 kph). They can lift objects as large as trains and hurl them to the ground, rip roofs off houses and whip out the furniture, suck up papers and photographs and drop them many miles away, and even strip clothes off a person's body. Tornadoes have hit almost every state in the US, but most of the world's tornadoes happen in the open prairies of the American Midwest. There, the tornado season normally lasts from May to October.

FLYING FISH
Tornadoes passing over lakes and sea may suck up fish and frogs, then drop them on dry land.

TORNADO ALLEY
In the center of the United States is an area known as Tornado Alley. It covers parts of Kansas, Oklahoma, and Missouri—the Great Plains. In the summer, cold air from Canada underrides warm, moist air from the Gulf of Mexico and hot, dry air from the Great Plains, causing great atmospheric instability. Eighty percent of the world's tornadoes occur here.

Tower of cloud called a thunderhead tops the supercell

Revolving mesocyclone sucks up dust from the ground

STORM CLOUDS
When a huge, dark storm cloud known as a supercell fills the sky, a tornado may be on the way. Strong winds moving in different directions inside the cloud create a region of low pressure beneath the cloud. Warm, moist air rushes into the updraft and rises to meet cold air higher up. The two air masses turn around each other to form a wide column of air called a mesocyclone.

1 FUNNEL APPEARS
The first signs of a mesocyclone are swirling dust at ground level and a funnel of water vapor extending down from the cloud. As warm, moist air from the atmosphere is sucked into the base of the mesocyclone, it spins upward, carrying dust with it.

2 COLUMN FORMS
The warm air rises and cools, forming water vapor that joins the swirling funnel. When the funnel touches the ground it becomes a tornado. As the tornado sucks up more dust, and more warm air cools to become water vapor, the tornado becomes clearly visible.

3 DYING DOWN
The tornado slows down as it runs out of moist, warm air at the bottom or when cool, dry air sinks from the cloud. Tornadoes can last from a few seconds to an hour or more, but most last about three minutes.

DUST DEVIL
As air rises in the hot desert, it can create a draft that begins to swirl, just like a tornado. This tower of whirling dust and sand, known as a dust devil, can reach 1.2 miles (2 km) high. Dust devils are less fierce than tornadoes, with wind speeds reaching only about 60 mph (100 kph).

TERRIFYING TWISTER
Inside the tornado's column, air whirls inward and upward, creating a flow called a vortex, at up to 300 mph (500 kph)—double the speed of the most powerful hurricanes. Pressure inside the vortex is so low that the twister sucks up items beneath it, like a vacuum cleaner. Tornadoes rarely travel more than 6 miles (10 km) before they run out of energy, but one twister may trigger another, leading to a terrifying tornado outbreak.

Wind speed is faster in narrow parts of the column

TORNADO DAMAGE
When people emerge from their homes after a tornado has passed through, they may find everything flattened. Ruined vehicles lie around, crushed by falling debris, or smashed by the twister. Trees can be snapped in two, and power lines trail from broken poles. Flimsy mobile homes are particularly at risk from tornado damage.

STORM CHASERS
When a severe storm develops, scientists known as storm chasers follow the storm to monitor its progress. A Doppler radar mounted on a truck allows them to watch for a vortex developing inside the storm clouds. But even storm chasers cannot predict a tornado more than 24 hours in advance.

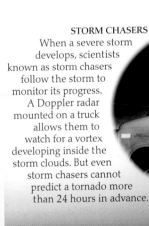

WATERSPOUT
A tornado over the ocean or a lake contains a column of condensed water, forming a pale waterspout. Although the wind speeds inside a waterspout are usually less than a tornado, the vortex is still powerful enough to lift a boat right out of the water.

Flood alert

WATER IS VITAL to survival—for drinking, washing, and growing crops. Rivers and seas provide food and transportation links to other places. But when a river bursts its banks, or huge storm waves sweep in from the sea, water becomes a deadly enemy. The force of the flooding river or sea can sweep away people and animals, and flatten poorly constructed buildings. In a historic city, buildings that have stood for centuries can be damaged, and valuable artwork destroyed. In steep landscapes, torrential rain can lead to a flash flood—a deadly surge of water that rises so rapidly that it can catch people completely unprepared.

RAINY SEASON
In India, children often celebrate the first rains of the monsoon season. The monsoon usually starts with a dramatic thunderstorm and torrential rain lasting several days. In spite of the flooding it brings, the monsoon is eagerly awaited, since it signals the end of the hot, humid season, and provides water for thirsty crops.

Flood plains of Lower Nile River

FERTILE FLOOD PLAINS
The ancient Egyptians depended on the Nile's annual flood across its flood plain—the flat land on either side of the river. When the waters receded, they left behind nutrient-rich silt which made the soil more fertile. Since 1970, the Aswan High Dam has reduced the Nile's flooding, and today's farmers have to use fertilizers on their fields.

Flooded farmhouses at
Machland, Austria, August 2002

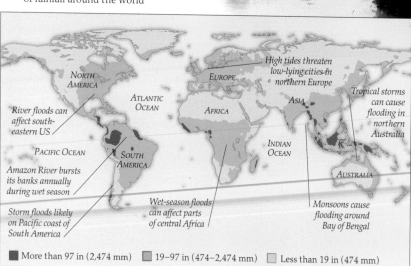

INLAND FLOODING
In 2002, after torrential rain in central Europe, the Danube, Elbe, and Vltava rivers flooded. Flood defenses failed and vast areas of the Czech Republic, Austria, and Germany were under water. In the Czech capital, Prague, floodwaters filled the underground subway system and severely damaged historic buildings. When rivers burst their banks in urban areas, floodwaters can turn towns into vast lakes, or rush down hills in flash floods.

Map showing the annual amount
of rainfall around the world

NORTH
AMERICA

ATLANTIC
OCEAN

EUROPE

High tides threaten
low-lying cities in
northern Europe

ASIA

Tropical storms
can cause
flooding in
northern
Australia

AFRICA

River floods can
affect south-
eastern US

PACIFIC OCEAN

SOUTH
AMERICA

INDIAN
OCEAN

Amazon River bursts
its banks annually
during wet season

AUSTRALIA

Storm floods likely
on Pacific coast of
South America

Wet-season floods
can affect parts
of central Africa

Monsoons cause
flooding around
Bay of Bengal

■ More than 97 in (2,474 mm)   ■ 19–97 in (474–2,474 mm)   □ Less than 19 in (474 mm)

THE WORLD'S RAINFALL
The average rainfall across the world is 40 in (100 cm) per year. But this is not evenly distributed. Many parts of the world have moderate rainfall, while others suffer droughts and some are regularly under water. The amount of rain a region receives depends on many factors including air temperature, the shape and size of the land mass, and season.

MELTING GLACIER
The gradual melting of frozen river ice or mountain glaciers is often so slow that it cannot cause a flood. Sometimes, as the ice begins to break up, floating chunks can pile up to form a dam across the river, causing the river to overflow upstream. When the ice dam cracks or bursts, the build-up of water is released downstream in an icy flash flood.

Sluice gates on Three Gorges Dam, Hubei Province, China

Pond formed by melted ice (meltwater)

DIVERTING THE WATERS
Along some rivers, engineers have built water channels called sluices to direct water away from flood-prone areas. River levels are monitored constantly as even slight rises upstream (near the river's source) may lead to a flood downstream (near the sea). When the sluice gates are opened, the excess water gushes through into a runoff lake.

Gates open to allow river traffic through

PROTECTING LONDON
London's Thames Barrier protects the city from flooding caused by the tidal Thames River. The barrier's gates close to prevent tidal surges from traveling upriver into the city center. Tidal rivers such as the Thames are at risk from floods due to unusually high tides, and storm surges.

Doppler radar dome receives returning radio waves

Red areas show approaching storm

Color codings for storm magnitude

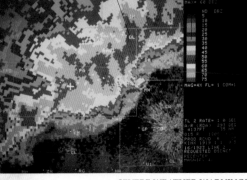

SEVERE WEATHER WARNINGS
Today, it is possible to make accurate weather forecasts using Doppler radar equipment. The system locates storms and measures their speed and direction by bouncing radio waves off clouds. This weather map, made from a Doppler radar readout, shows a severe thunderstorm in Kansas.

Raging waters

When a flood strikes, roads become impassable, either too deep in water for vehicles to travel, or washed away by the floodwaters. With no way to escape the flood, people climb higher and higher as the waters rise, first to the upper stories of buildings, then onto roofs or in high trees. There, they wait for rescuers to arrive in boats or helicopters. One way to protect people from the danger of flooding would be to stop building homes on flood plains. But many large cities already exist on flood plains. In heavily populated, low-lying countries, such as Bangladesh and the Netherlands, there is not enough higher ground.

Ball of smoking incense

NOAH'S ARK
In the Bible story, Noah's ark floated on a flood caused by 40 days of heavy rain. Noah and his passengers stayed on the ark for a year until the floodwaters dried up.

THE RIGHT RAIN
In ancient times, as today, rain was vital to water crops, but storms could destroy them—and wreck villages. The Mayan people made offerings to Chac, their god of rain, in the hope that he would provide rain but keep floods at bay.

The usual course of the Yangtze River

Houses under 3 ft (1 m) of water

CONTROLLING THE YANGTZE RIVER
The banks of China's Yangtze River burst regularly after heavy rain, killing thousands of people in some years. One of the worst floods occurred in August 2002, when some 900,000 people were displaced. Ten years earlier, the Chinese government had begun work on the Three Gorges Dam (the world's largest dam), designed to control the flooding. The dam itself was finished in 2006, but it has caused several other problems, such as local ground tremors.

ESCAPING THE WATER

As the waters of the Mississippi and its tributaries rose in 1993, people climbed on to roofs and trees to escape the rising floodwater. About 45 people died in the floods and nearly 70,000 were left homeless.

Rescue worker helps a woman climb down from the roof of her home into a boat

ROAD TO NOWHERE

This collapsed bridge in Quincy, Illinois, became submerged when the largest river in the United States, the Mississippi, and its tributary the Missouri, flooded in 1993. An area of over 31,000 sq miles (80,000 sq km) was under water. The devastating floods occurred when dams and levees burst following 10 times the usual amount of spring rainfall on the central plains.

Aerial view of swamped cars near Wangaratta, Australia

SWIRLING WATERS

Scrapped cars sit deep in muddy floodwater after heavy rain swept across southeastern Australia in September 2010. The state of Victoria suffered its worst floods in a decade, forcing the evacuation of several cities and cutting the electricity supplies to at least 40,000 homes. Within three months, another series of floods devastated the northeastern Australian state of Queensland.

Container for emergency food ration

LIVING WITH FLOODS

Bangladeshi women and children line up, waist-deep in floodwater, for emergency supplies. Low-lying Bangladesh lies between two huge rivers, the Ganges and the Brahmaputra, and its people are accustomed to flooding every year during the monsoon. But in 1997–1998, the weather pattern called El Niño triggered such a huge increase in the monsoon rain that two-thirds of the country was inundated. Ten million people lost their homes.

Drought and famine

It is hard to tell exactly when a drought starts. When there is much less rain than usual, the soil gradually dries out and plants begin to die. When water levels drop and cracks appear in dry lakes and riverbeds, the drought is well under way. If it continues, the drought may cause a famine and people and animals starve. The best preparation for drought is to store water in reservoirs or tanks when there is plenty, but the driest places never have enough water. In such places, drought cannot be prevented, but the famine that often follows can, providing that water supplies, food resources, and aid are supplied before people begin to suffer.

VANISHING SEA
The Aral Sea between Kazakhstan and Uzbekistan had shrunk to just 10 percent of its original area by 2007 and is still shrinking, despite efforts to conserve the relatively small northern section. The sea has become far more salty, too, killing the fish that once provided three percent of the Soviet Union's total catch.

Boat grounded on sands that were once under the Aral Sea

UNDERGROUND WATER
In 2003, Gujarat in India suffered its worst drought in 10 years. The only water left was to be found in deep wells such as this one. People had to travel long distances, often on foot, and wait their turn for just a few pots of water. When drought dries up the soil and surface water, groundwater still flows deep under the ground, trapped by hard layers of rock. Deep wells tap into this resource.

Field of dried-out sunflowers in Spain

THIRSTY CROPS
In a drought, the first people to suffer are often farmers, when crops such as these sunflowers die. In wealthy countries, other people may be affected when water shortages lead to bans on watering lawns. However, there is usually enough water stored in reservoirs for drinking and washing until rain replenishes water supplies.

HOLDING BACK THE DESERT
Rainfall is unpredictable on the fringes of deserts, such as in Niger on the edge of the Sahara Desert. During droughts, the sand dunes can spread, burying surrounding towns and farms. To help stop this, farmers plant the dunes with crops such as millet, which binds the sand together and stops it from blowing toward the fields.

DUST BOWL
During the 1930s, a severe drought hit the American Great Plains. Intensive farming had robbed the soil of nutrients and, when drought struck, the soil turned to dust and blew away. The region became known as the Dust Bowl. Crop failures and famine soon followed the drought and, by 1937, half a million people had abandoned their farms.

Burial mounds

Brick lining stops soil from collapsing into the well

Metal pots lowered on ropes to reach groundwater

Animal carcass, a common sight during severe droughts

FAMINE
When drought hit the African countries of Sudan and Ethiopia in 1984–85, first crops failed and then livestock began to starve. With neither crops nor livestock, the people had no food and no income to buy any, and they too began to starve. In the severe famine that followed, 450,000 people in the region died.

REFUGEE CAMP
In the worst droughts, people are forced to leave their homes and gather in refugee camps. Here, they can receive food and shelter—this camp in Mogadishu is serving cooked meals to Somali families, until the drought lifts and they can return to their land. Aid organizations, such as Doctors Without Borders and UNICEF, supply clean water, food, medicines, and shelter to the refugees.

49

Wildfire

Forest fire warning

FROM THE FIRST FLICKER of flame in dry grass, a wildfire spreads rapidly across the countryside. Flames leap from tree to tree and burning embers fly about in the wind, igniting more vegetation, while terrified animals flee from the oncoming flames. Also known as bush fires or forest fires, wildfires are a regular occurrence during the long, dry summers in the forests of Australia, California, and southern Europe. Today, wildfires are sometimes left to burn themselves out and the landscape to regenerate naturally. However, when a wildfire gets out of control, firefighters battle to stop the fire destroying whole wildernesses or spreading to built-up areas.

Dark red areas are the hottest, showing ground temperatures above 131°F (55°C)

Cool blue-green area is the Pacific Ocean

HEATWAVE
This thermal satellite image shows ground temperatures in California during a heatwave in May 2004. The heatwave led to an early start to the wildfire season. Wildfires are worst in very hot years when lack of rain dries out the vegetation, providing easily ignitable fuel for the fires.

LIGHTNING BOLT
About half of all wildfires are started by people, either deliberately or accidentally; the rest start naturally. The spark that lights most natural wildfires is a bolt of lightning during a summer storm. Dry vegetation provides the fuel a fire needs and storm winds fan the flames. Within minutes, a landscape can be transformed.

Thick, choking smoke rises from a land-clearance fire

BLACK SATURDAY
In early 2009, southeastern Australia was struck by a series of disastrous wildfires. They started on Saturday, February 7, when a combination of extremely hot weather and tinder-dry bush sparked dozens of blazes across the country. Wildfire is a regular event in Australia, but these were extreme. The intense heat generated deadly firestorms that devoured everything in their path, and a single firestorm north of Melbourne claimed 120 lives. Altogether, the fires killed 173 people—the worst-ever death toll from wildfire in Australian history. Not surprisingly, the day when they started is now known as Black Saturday.

FARMERS' FIRES
In the rainforests of Southeast Asia and South America, farmers clear land by burning down trees and undergrowth. They grow crops on the land for a few years and then leave it to become forest again. But farmers' fires are difficult to control, and they sometimes grow into dangerous wildfires.

Indian Ocean

Island of Borneo

Smoke from wildfires

Red dots show fires still burning

NEW GROWTH

Wildfires are a vital part of the life cycle of these North American lodgepole pines. These trees release their seeds only in the intense heat of a fire. Forest fires can be beneficial to other plants and trees, too. They clear the forest floor for new seedlings to grow, return nutrients to the soil, and kill off pests and diseases.

AN ISLAND BURNS

Throughout the summer of 2002, glowing fires and a blanket of smoke across Borneo, Southeast Asia, were clearly visible from space. Logging companies started the fires deliberately to clear parts of the rainforest, but they rapidly got out of hand. The fires, which also struck the nearby island of Sumatra, destroyed an area of forest half the size of Switzerland. Even after a rainforest fire has been put out, the layer of peat under the forest continues to smoulder and can reignite the flames.

Rising hot air sucks in more air at the bottom, fueling the fire with oxygen

Fighting fires

FIRE ENGINE
In urban areas, fire engines can connect their hoses to fire hydrants for water to douse the flames. In the wilderness, firefighters drive tanks of water to the scene of the fire, or pump it from nearby water sources.

IT MAY TAKE more than a week for firefighters, working on the ground and in the air, to bring a major wildfire under control. In the most remote regions, firefighters may have to battle their way to the heart of the fire through leaping flames, falling trees, choking smoke, and nearly 1,000°F (500°C) temperatures. But some wildfires are unstoppable. In 1997, after months of drought, more than 100 fires were blazing among the rainforests of Indonesia. Firefighting experts flew in from around the world, but many fires could not be brought under control. At last, the long-awaited monsoon rains fell, extinguishing the flames until the next year's wildfire season.

Cruise speed is 126 mph (203 kph)

Helicopter carries one pilot, two fire chiefs, and eight firefighters

FIGHTING FIRES
Firefighters use various methods to tackle wildfires. They spray water or chemicals onto the burning vegetation to lower its temperature and make the fuel less flammable. They may cut down or burn vegetation around the area where the fire is heading so that the fire runs out of fuel. Firefighters may also use diggers to create wide, bare trenches that the flames cannot leap over.

CHOKING SMOG
Raging fires consumed over 750,000 acres (300,000 hectares) of forest in Southeast Asia in 1997. The smoke created a gray haze of choking smog that affected more than 70 million people. In some areas, one day's exposure to the polluted air was equivalent to smoking dozens of cigarettes. Protective masks were worn by many people in an attempt to minimize damage to the lungs.

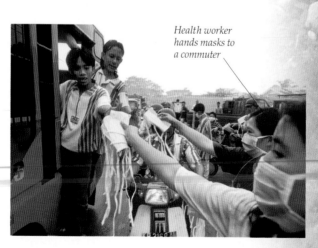

Health worker hands masks to a commuter

Sparks shoot out as the tree ignites

FLAMING TREE
Australian *Eucalyptus* trees are rich in natural oils, which prevent them from drying out in the arid climate. But it makes them very flammable. In the hot, dry Australian summer, the intense heat of an approaching fire can cause the trees to ignite spontaneously. When the fire is over, new growth can spring from beneath the charred bark, and the fire-resistant *Eucalyptus* seeds soon germinate in the ash-rich soil.

Tank can hold 300 gallons (1,360 litres) of water or foam

Brightly colored, fire-resistant clothing

FIGHTING BUSHFIRES
In 2002, wildfires reached the fringes of urban areas in New South Wales, Australia. Firefighters struggled to turn back the flames, but 170 homes were destroyed. Around the Australian bush, firefighters are now carrying out regular, controlled burnings to clear the dry undergrowth. This helps to prevent major fires.

High collar protects neck from branches during jump

Water turned to steam by the heat of the flames

DOUSING THE FLAMES
Wildfires are an annual hazard to people living near forested areas of southern California. In 2004 alone, over 5,500 fires spread across 168,000 acres (68,000 hectares) of the state, destroying more than 1,000 buildings. The California fire service has specially adapted helicopters that can scoop or suck up water from a nearby water source, such as a lake. The load is dumped onto the hottest part of the fire or onto surrounding vegetation to make it less likely to catch fire.

SMOKEJUMPERS
In remote areas, firefighters known as smokejumpers parachute in to tackle small fires before they can spread. Smokejumpers cannot parachute with much equipment, so pumps and heavy tools are dropped separately. When the job is done, the smokejumpers often have to hike out of the area carrying all the equipment with them.

Helmet with heavy mesh face mask

Gearbag

Climate change

OVER MILLIONS OF YEARS, the Earth's climate has swung from freezing ice ages to swelteringly hot periods many times. Long-term climate change is caused by variations in the Sun's heat output, in the tilt of the Earth, and in the distance between the Earth and Sun as the two move through space. For about the last 100 years, our planet has been growing warmer but, in the last few decades, the rate of change has increased dramatically. Most scientists believe that this global warming is largely due to the enormous volumes of polluting gases released by burning fossil fuels such as coal. Global warming will probably cause more extreme weather, with fiercer storms and deadlier droughts.

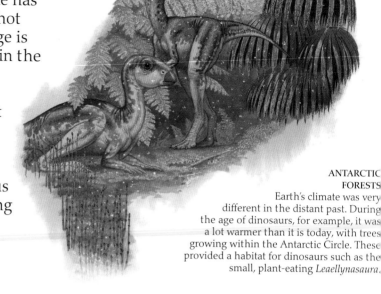

ANTARCTIC FORESTS
Earth's climate was very different in the distant past. During the age of dinosaurs, for example, it was a lot warmer than it is today, with trees growing within the Antarctic Circle. These provided a habitat for dinosaurs such as the small, plant-eating *Leaellynasaura*.

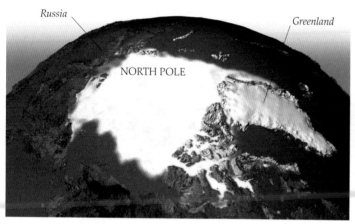

Russia　　　　　　　*Greenland*
NORTH POLE

ARCTIC SEA ICE, 1979
One of the clearest effects of global warming is the reduced extent of sea ice (frozen sea water) in the Arctic. This satellite image shows the extent of the Arctic summer sea ice in 1979, around the North Pole. An ice sheet covers much of the eastern coast of Greenland and sea ice stretches as far as the northern coast of Russia.

POLAR HABITAT UNDER THREAT
Reduction in the sea ice threatens the survival of polar bears, because they spend much of their lives traveling across the ice, hunting for seals in the Arctic waters. Warmer conditions in the Arctic may mean that most of the floating ice sheet will become a seasonal feature, melting in summer and reforming in winter. As the temperature rises, massive cracks appear in the polar sea ice. Gradually, chunks of ice break off and float away.

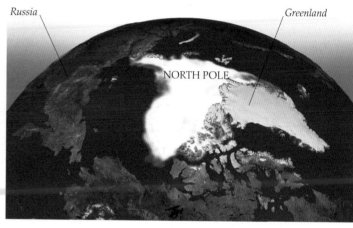

Russia　　　　　　　*Greenland*
NORTH POLE

ARCTIC SEA ICE, 2007
This satellite image clearly shows how much the Arctic summer sea ice sheet had shrank in 2007 when it reached an all-time low. Some scientists estimate that it could melt away altogether in the summer of 2030, if not before. Meanwhile, the fringes of the Greenland ice sheet are getting thinner, and the extra meltwater flowing off the land has already raised sea levels enough to threaten many low-lying islands and coasts.

Drifting chunks of ice melt faster than the solid ice sheet

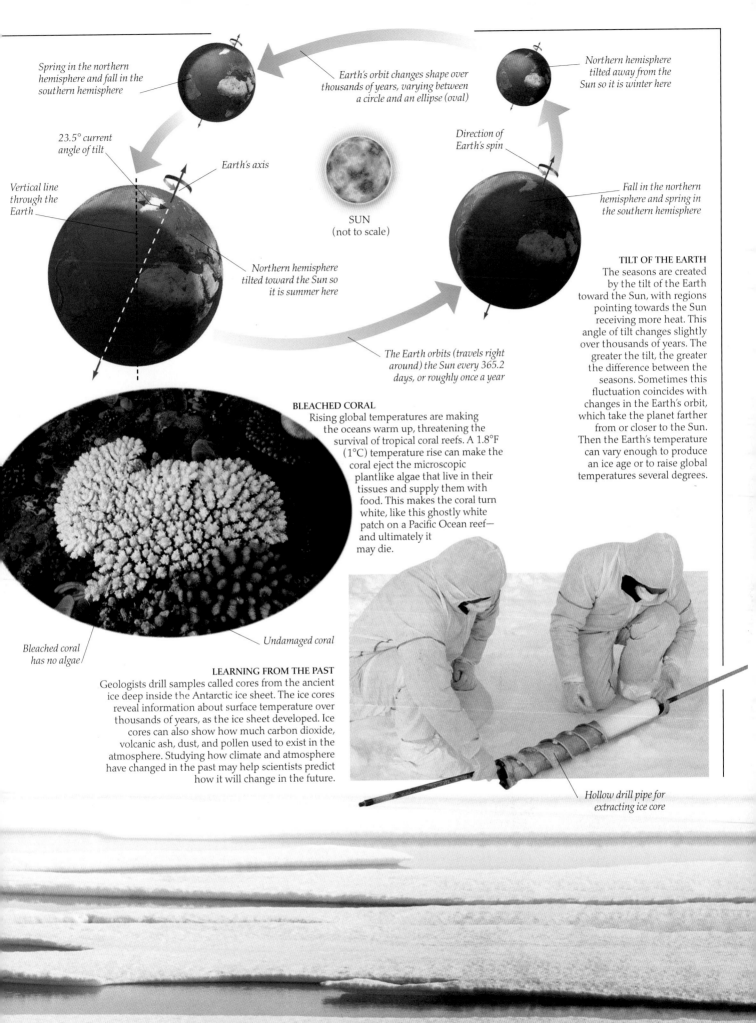

Spring in the northern hemisphere and fall in the southern hemisphere

Earth's orbit changes shape over thousands of years, varying between a circle and an ellipse (oval)

Northern hemisphere tilted away from the Sun so it is winter here

23.5° current angle of tilt

Earth's axis

Direction of Earth's spin

Vertical line through the Earth

SUN
(not to scale)

Northern hemisphere tilted toward the Sun so it is summer here

Fall in the northern hemisphere and spring in the southern hemisphere

TILT OF THE EARTH
The seasons are created by the tilt of the Earth toward the Sun, with regions pointing towards the Sun receiving more heat. This angle of tilt changes slightly over thousands of years. The greater the tilt, the greater the difference between the seasons. Sometimes this fluctuation coincides with changes in the Earth's orbit, which take the planet farther from or closer to the Sun. Then the Earth's temperature can vary enough to produce an ice age or to raise global temperatures several degrees.

The Earth orbits (travels right around) the Sun every 365.2 days, or roughly once a year

BLEACHED CORAL
Rising global temperatures are making the oceans warm up, threatening the survival of tropical coral reefs. A 1.8°F (1°C) temperature rise can make the coral eject the microscopic plantlike algae that live in their tissues and supply them with food. This makes the coral turn white, like this ghostly white patch on a Pacific Ocean reef— and ultimately it may die.

Undamaged coral

Bleached coral has no algae

LEARNING FROM THE PAST
Geologists drill samples called cores from the ancient ice deep inside the Antarctic ice sheet. The ice cores reveal information about surface temperature over thousands of years, as the ice sheet developed. Ice cores can also show how much carbon dioxide, volcanic ash, dust, and pollen used to exist in the atmosphere. Studying how climate and atmosphere have changed in the past may help scientists predict how it will change in the future.

Hollow drill pipe for extracting ice core

Unnatural disasters

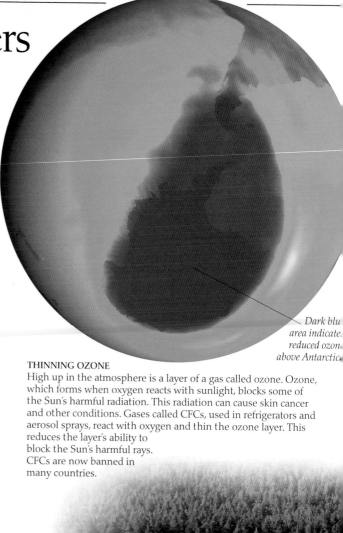

Pollution monitor

SOME DISASTERS are not caused by the natural world, but by its exploitation. Waste fumes from vehicles and from industry pollute the air we breathe. Burning fossil fuels (coal, oil, and gas) provides us with power, but also releases gases into the atmosphere that can cause climate change. Supplies of these fuels are dwindling fast, but the amount of power we use continues to increase. Forests are being cut down for lumber and farmland, and oceans are being emptied of fish to provide food. Scientists warn that we urgently need to change the way we treat our planet. Cutting our use of natural resources and our production of pollution requires the agreement of the world's governments and action by ordinary people.

Dark blu[e] area indicate[s] reduced ozon[e] above Antarctic[a]

THINNING OZONE

High up in the atmosphere is a layer of a gas called ozone. Ozone, which forms when oxygen reacts with sunlight, blocks some of the Sun's harmful radiation. This radiation can cause skin cancer and other conditions. Gases called CFCs, used in refrigerators and aerosol sprays, react with oxygen and thin the ozone layer. This reduces the layer's ability to block the Sun's harmful rays. CFCs are now banned in many countries.

Redwood forest, northern California

DEFORESTATION

Today, forests are being cut down faster than they are being replaced. Their trees provide lumber and, cleared of trees, the land can be used for farms and homes. But forests are vital to life on Earth. As part of the process called photosynthesis, trees absorb carbon dioxide, and produce oxygen for animals to breathe. Deforestation can lead to the extinction of plants and animals by destroying their wild habitats.

POISONING THE AIR

Like many of the world's big cities, on hot days Santiago in Chile is shrouded in a choking cloud of smog. This smog is a sooty fog containing a mixture of harmful gases, including carbon monoxide, produced when vehicle exhaust fumes react with sunlight. The polluted air can aggravate conditions such as asthma and bronchitis and cause eye irritations.

In China, people flee a duststorm in a region suffering desertification

DESERTIFICATION

On the edges of deserts, years can go by with little or no rainfall. When these areas are heavily populated, the vegetation is stripped away, usually for animal feed, faster than it can regrow. Soon desertification, the spread of desert conditions, sets in and the soil turns to barren dust. Along the edges of Asian and African deserts, millions of the world's poorest people are losing their land and their livelihoods as the deserts spread.

Catch of herring on a Norwegian trawler

DWINDLING RESOURCES

Factory trawlers like this can catch and process several hundred tons of fish a day. Fish count for 10 percent of the protein eaten by humans worldwide and, as the world population grows, the demand for fish grows, too. Fish stocks are falling rapidly around the world and some species face extinction.

Gray areas show coral damaged by dynamite

Cutting down a large area of trees can be very harmful to wildlife

BLAST FISHING

Among the world's most beautiful and productive environments, coral reefs are being damaged by an extraordinarily destructive form of fishing—blasting fish out of the water with dynamite. In parts of the developing world, blast fishing is used as a cheap, quick way to harvest fish, but it kills the coral beneath the shallow waters. It can take more than 20 years before the coral begins to recover.

ACID RAIN

These lifeless trees may look as if they have been hit by drought—in fact, acid rain has killed them. Burning fossil fuels releases nitrogen and sulfur oxides, which form acids in the atmosphere. The wind carries these acids far from the cities and industries that produce them, until they fall as acid rain, killing trees and poisoning rivers.

Infectious diseases

THE DEADLIEST DISASTERS are not due to wild weather or the movements of the Earth. They are caused by organisms so tiny that they can be seen only under powerful microscopes. Infectious diseases, including malaria, cholera, tuberculosis, and AIDS, are responsible for more than 13 million premature deaths throughout the world each year. These diseases are caused by bacteria, fungi, viruses, and other microorganisms, which invade the body through cuts, via insect bites, through our mouths and noses as we breathe, and in the food and beverages we consume. Some can even kill by destroying the crops we depend on for food.

Piercing sucking mouthparts adapted to feed on blood

DEADLY FLEA
In the 14th century, the bubonic plague struck Asia and Europe, killing 40 million people. The Black Death, as it was known, was spread by the black rats that swarmed the streets. The rats were hosts for the carriers—fleas. When an infected flea bit a human, its saliva transmitted the bacteria that causes the plague.

Long hind legs for jumping from host to host

INFECTIOUS DROPLETS
Disease-carrying organisms can be spread in droplets of water that explode from the mouth or nose in a sneeze. The relatively harmless common cold is spread this way, but so are much more serious diseases, such as smallpox and tuberculosis.

Air rushes from the lungs at 95 mph (150 kph)

Rwandan refugees skim a mud puddle for their drinking water

DIRTY WATER
In the aftermath of wars and natural disasters, when refugees are gathered in temporary camps with limited supplies of clean water, one of the biggest threats to health is an outbreak of cholera. This deadly infection is caused by bacteria that thrive in dirty water. It causes acute diarrhea and vomiting, which can quickly lead to severe dehydration.

POWER OF THE MICROSCOPE
Scientists can identify and study the microorganisms that cause disease using microscopes. This scanning electron microscope can magnify up to 250,000 times. It works by bouncing a beam of electrons off a sample to create a black-and-white 3-D image—color is added by a computer. Dutch scientist Anton van Leeuwenhoek (1632–1723) was the first to observe tiny living organisms such as bacteria and blood cells under a microscope.

Potato blight mold spot

POTATO BLIGHT
This picture, produced by a scanning electron microscope, shows a tiny fungus, called *Phytophthora infestans*. Fungi are tiny plantlike organisms that feed on dead or living plants and animals. *Phytophthora infestans* causes potato blight, which rots the vegetable. Potato blight decimated the potato crop across Europe in the 1840s, and led to starvation and death for a million people in Ireland, where potatoes were the major food crop.

Viewing port, for observing sample

Protein coat locks on to host cell, allowing it to be invaded

VIRUSES
This scanning electron micrograph shows the variola virus that causes smallpox. Much smaller than a bacterium, a virus is a tiny package of genetic material surrounded by a protein shell. Viruses cause diseases—from smallpox and AIDS to the common cold—by invading a host's cells with the protein on their shells, then injecting their own genetic material into the cells.

The virus's instructions for copying itself are contained in its DNA

Pressure-resistant shell encloses a vacuum chamber in which electrons bombard the sample

SMALLPOX SCARRING
This Nigerian wooden statue of the Spirit of Smallpox is covered in spots which represent the smallpox rash. Smallpox is no longer a threat, but it was a highly infectious disease which left victims covered in unsightly scars—if they were lucky enough to survive. There was no treatment for smallpox once it was contracted.

Epidemic

AN OUTBREAK OF A DISEASE that spreads rapidly through the population is known as an epidemic. When it begins to affect vast numbers of people over a wide area, it becomes a pandemic. Today, the global AIDS pandemic is perhaps the most serious health threat facing the world. Some epidemics can be prevented by killing the disease-carrying organisms, such as mosquitoes. Epidemics of diseases such as measles and smallpox can be avoided by vaccination. Health education can help prevent the spread of infections such as AIDS. Outbreaks of cholera and other waterborne diseases can be halted, before they become epidemics, as long as people live in sanitary conditions and have access to clean water.

FLU RESEARCH
These sample blocks contain lung and brain tissue from victims of the 1918–20 influenza (flu) pandemic, which killed 25–50 million people worldwide. Researchers hope to isolate the flu virus from the samples to discover why this strain of flu was so deadly. Flu viruses are difficult to treat because they can mutate into different forms.

Names of victims of the flu pandemic

VACCINATING THE WORLD
After smallpox caused two million deaths in 1967, the World Health Organization began a mass vaccination program in an attempt to eliminate the disease. A vaccination is a weak or dead form of the disease-causing organism that when injected into the body stimulates the immune system to build up a resistance. Health workers traveled to the remote places of the world and carried out house-to-house searches to reach everyone who was at risk. The strategy was eventually successful and, in 1980, smallpox became the only major infectious human disease to be eradicated completely.

PLAGUE OUTBREAK
When pneumonic plague killed 51 people in Surat, western India, in 1994, hundreds of thousands of people fled in terror. Garbage was cleared from the streets and burned to destroy the disease-carrying rats. Pneumonic plague infects the lungs, but is caused by the same bacteria as the glandular disease bubonic plague, which swept Europe in the 1300s.

Multishot inoculation gun forces vaccine through the skin at high pressure, without a needle

CONTROLLING MALARIA
On the tiny island of Car Nicobar in the Bay of Bengal, an aid worker sprays stagnant water with chemicals to kill the mosquito larvae. The 2004 Asian tsunami left behind a lot of stagnant water, creating breeding grounds for mosquitoes that could cause malaria outbreaks.

MOSQUITO LARVAE
Mosquito eggs hatch into larvae in water, and then develop into winged adults. The adult females feed on the blood of mammals, spreading diseases including malaria and dengue fever. Scientists have not yet found a way to prevent mosquitoes from breeding, so the mosquito larvae are killed to help prevent the spread of these diseases.

Disposable gloves, to help prevent spreading infection

INFECTION CONTROL
Hygiene is one of the most important weapons in the fight against potentially lethal microorganisms, which thrive in dirty conditions. Some of these, such as MRSA, have developed a resistance to most antibiotics, so treating them is very difficult.

HOSPITAL INFECTION
When MRSA (Methicillin-resistant *Staphylococcus aureus*) bacteria are passed on to a hospital patient through a wound or a dirty medical tube, they can cause a severe infection. Patients found to be carrying MRSA are isolated to prevent the infection from spreading. They are treated with powerful antibiotics but, in the frailest patients, MRSA can be fatal.

MRSA
bacteria

HIV, colored red, invades a blood cell

HIV AND AIDS
The Human Immunodeficiency Virus (HIV), which causes AIDS (Acquired Immune Deficiency Syndrome), kills white blood cells, multiplies, and spreads. As more and more blood cells are destroyed, the body loses the ability to fight off infections. Thirty-six million people worldwide are infected with HIV, and AIDS is fast becoming one of the biggest killers in history.

White blood cell, colored green in this image

AIDS EDUCATORS
World AIDS day is commemorated by lighting candles for victims of the disease. Campaigners around the world are trying to educate people about AIDS to help prevent its spread. There is no cure for AIDS, and many people in the developing world do not have access to the drugs that can control the disease.

61

Future disasters

As THE PLANET becomes more heavily populated, disasters such as volcanoes and tsunamis are more likely to cause catastrophic loss of life. The area affected by disasters may also be much greater—scientists fear a huge volcanic eruption in the US, and a mega-tsunami from the Canary Islands, although they hope these are a long way in the future. In our lifetimes, disaster is more likely to strike in the form of a new global pandemic, which could wipe out millions. There is one disaster capable of destroying all life on Earth in a single blow—a Near Earth Object (NEO) such as a huge asteroid or comet crashing into our planet.

SUPERVOLCANO
Below Yellowstone National Park in Wyoming a massive magma chamber heats the water that bursts from the famous geysers. If enough pressure built up in the magma chamber, it could cause the biggest volcanic eruption in recorded history, destroying much of the US, and blasting enough ash into the air to cool the Earth. Some scientists warn that an eruption at Yellowstone is now overdue.

KILLER FLU
When diseases develop strains capable of infecting more than one species, they can become very potent. Avian influenza, or bird flu, is a disease of poultry, but in Hong Kong in 1997 it began infecting humans. In 2009, Mexico saw a human outbreak of swine flu, which usually infects pigs. Either could become a mass killer.

Mount Vesuvius

DEVASTATION OF ITALY
If Italy's Mount Vesuvius exploded in a massive volcanic eruption today, the effect would be far more devastating than when the volcano destroyed Pompeii in 79 CE. The south of Italy is now the most densely populated high-risk volcanic area on Earth. Six towns along the volcano's southern flank would be in danger, including the city of Naples, which has a population of one million people.

GOING GLOBAL
When bird flu broke out in China, poultry workers were careful to avoid infection. Normally, the virus is spread only by contact with birds, but it can develop a strain that spreads from one person to another. The same is true of swine flu—the virus that killed up to 100 million people in 1918–1919. Modern travelers would soon carry it worldwide, and since new strains do not respond to existing vaccines, the result could be a global pandemic.

MEGA-TSUNAMI

Some scientists calculate that a volcanic eruption could send the western half of the island of La Palma, one of Spain's Canary Islands, crashing into the sea. The 500-billion-ton landslide could send a mega-tsunami racing across the Atlantic to engulf the East Coast of the US, from New York to Miami, with waves 65 ft (20 m) high.

First 4 ft (1.2 m) reflecting telescope

Second 4 ft (1.2 m) reflecting telescope

The Cumbre Vieja ridge could collapse into the sea

Influenza virus particles shown in red

Culture cells used in virus research shown in blue

Assembly rotates on its base, enabling the two telescopes to track objects

Artist's impression of the asteroid or comet strike that destroyed the dinosaurs

TRACKING THE SKIES

Optical telescopes, such as this twin telescope from Maui Observatory in Hawaii, can track the movement of Near Earth Objects (NEOs) that could collide with Earth. NASA currently keeps track of 1,855 NEOs—none of them is heading for Earth just yet. The impact of an object half a mile (1 km) wide would destroy everything within 300 miles (500 km).

COLLISION COURSE

Powerful evidence suggests that 65 million years ago a huge object 6 miles (10 km) wide hit Mexico's Yucatan Peninsula. The impact produced a mega-tsunami, with waves half a mile (1 km) high. A cloud of water vapor and dust rose high into the atmosphere, blocking out the Sun and creating a long global winter. It is thought that this triggered a series of events that brought about the extinction of the giant dinosaurs and two-thirds of other animal species. To protect the Earth from any Near Earth Object (NEO) that might threaten disaster on a similar scale, scientists are searching for a way to destroy these objects with nuclear warheads, or push them off course by firing missiles at them.

Did you know?

AMAZING FACTS

So many volcanoes occur around the rim of the Pacific Plate that this zone is known as the Ring of Fire.

In 1902, Meteor Crater, Arizona, was the first crater on Earth to be recognized as being created by an impact. Before this, people thought the feature was the remains of an ancient volcano.

Forest fires clear trees and shrubs from the ground. Fresh seedlings of California's giant sequoias flourish after the fire because they have the space and access to sunlight they need to grow. The mature sequoia's thick, spongy bark protects the living part of the trunk from burning, and its deep roots reach water far underground. No wonder some of these trees live to be more than 3,000 years old.

Burned giant sequoia, California

Rain may fall only once every eight years in parts of the Sahara Desert.

About 150,000 noticeable earthquakes happen every year. More than a million are detected by seismograms.

Rain darkens the desert sands

Scientists used to call tsunamis seismic sea waves because they thought they were caused only by earthquakes. But these waves can also be caused by impacts on the water's surface, so scientists now use the name tsunami, or harbor wave.

If lightning strikes a tree, the moisture inside may boil, blowing the tree to pieces.

Thunder is the sound of air around a bolt of lightning exploding as it is heated to 54,000°F (30,000°C) in less than a second.

For a hurricane to develop out over the sea, the sea temperature must be no lower than 80°F (27°C).

In January 1974, a tornado in McComb, Mississippi, threw three buses over a 7-ft- (2-m-) high wall.

In December 1952, 4,000 people died in London's smog, caused largely by burning coal as a heating fuel.

From 1550 to 1850, there were fewer solar flares and sunspots on the Sun than usual, showing that the Sun emitted slightly less heat. This coincided with a cooler period in the Earth's history known as the Little Ice Age.

The 2004 Asian tsunami washed away centuries of sand from the buried ruins of a 1,200-year old city at Mahabalipuram, southern India.

The size of the seasonal hole in the ozone layer over Antarctica peaked in 2000, at 11.3 million sq miles (29.2 million sq km). The hole is gradually getting smaller.

Drought conditions vary from place to place, depending on how much rain is normal for the place and the season. In the United States, a drought is declared after 21 days with less than 30 percent of normal rainfall. In the Sahara Desert, it takes two years without rain before a drought is declared.

If you are caught out in the open when a tornado strikes, lie down flat on the ground in a hollow or low-lying area with your hands over your head, until it passes.

The oldest rocks on land are about 3.5 billion years old, but the oldest rocks on the ocean floor are about 200 million years old. That is because new seafloor is being added where plates pull apart, while old seafloor is being subducted elsewhere.

If you breathed in the gas ozone, it would damage your lungs, but the ozone layer high up in the atmosphere is vital to screen out harmful radiation.

More earthquakes happen in the northern hemisphere than in the southern hemisphere.

When the Xiangjiang River in China flooded in August 2002, some residents of the city of Changsha had to move out of their flooded homes to live on a staircase leading to a bridge. The only way people could move around the city was by boat.

Flooding in Changsha, China

On December 26, 2004, a 10-year old British girl noticed the water was receding at Maikhao Beach, Phuket, Thailand. She had learned about tsunamis in a school geography class, and realized that a tsunami was about to happen. With the help of her parents, she warned people to leave the beach, and the evacuation saved 100 lives.

Medieval doctors had no idea how to cure the plague. Some put dried toads on the patient's buboes (swellings) to draw out the poison. Others tried to burn the buboes away with red-hot irons.

QUESTIONS AND ANSWERS

Q How far can lightning travel?

A Lightning can travel more than 6 miles (10 km). So, even if a storm is not overhead, you might get struck by lightning.

Q How are hurricane names decided?

A Hurricanes are given a name from a list drawn up several years in advance. Each new hurricane begins with the next letter of the alphabet, and male and female names alternate. After a devasting hurricane happens, its name is dropped. Typhoons have a different naming system.

Searching for avalanche survivors in Switzerland, 2002

Q How are avalanche survivors found?

A After an avalanche, teams of rescue workers move across the soft, fallen snow, gently probing with long sticks. If the stick meets an obstruction, the rescuers dig in that spot to see if someone is buried there. Some skiers carry electronic devices that signal their position to rescuers if an avalanche strikes.

Q What is smog?

A Smog is a mixture of smoke and fog. It is worst when pollutants accumulate in a shallow layer of cold air trapped under a lid of warmer air. Cities situated in a bowl surrounded by hills, such as Los Angeles and Mexico City, are more prone to smog because low-level air is sheltered from winds and a warm-air lid can readily settle over it.

Q How did scientists figure out that continents move around the Earth?

A In 1915, after noticing that the continent of South America looked as if it would fit against the western side of Africa, German scientist Alfred Wegener stated that today's continents were once part of a single landmass. It took over 30 years before his theory was generally accepted.

Q What was the world's worst-ever pandemic?

A The influenza epidemic of 1918 to 1920 killed 25–50 million people worldwide, and possibly far more.

Q Is it possible to harness the energy of a volcano?

A In volcanically active countries such as Iceland and New Zealand, power plants pump water down into the Earth's crust. Burning hot magma turns the water into steam, which rises and turns turbines that generate electricity. This type of power is known as geothermal energy.

Q In which direction do tornadoes spin?

A Tornadoes in the northern hemisphere spin counterclockwise, while in the southern hemisphere they spin clockwise.

Q Why is the weather pattern that switches the direction of warm water currents in the Pacific Ocean called El Niño?

A El Niño means "Christ Child" in Spanish. The weather pattern is named after the seasonal change in ocean currents off Peru that normally occurs around Christmas.

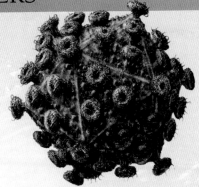

Particle of the HIV virus

Record Breakers

HEAVIEST HAILSTONES
In 1986, huge hailstones weighing more than 2¼ lb (1 kg) fell in Gopalganj, Bangladesh.

MOST VOLCANOES
Indonesia has more volcanoes than any other country, with 130 active volcanoes and another 270 that are either dormant or extinct.

MOST EXPENSIVE NATURAL DISASTER
The 2011 Japanese tsunami is the most expensive natural disaster to date.

WORST RECORDED LIGHTNING STRIKE
In December 1963, lightning struck an aircraft over Maryland that crashed, killing 81 people.

FASTEST AVALANCHE
In 1980, the volcanic eruption of Mount St. Helens, Washington, triggered the fastest recorded avalanche, with speeds of 250 mph (402 kph).

Storm waves caused by El Niño strike Malibu, California, 1983

Timeline

Black Death, London (1348)

THIS TIMELINE OUTLINES some of the most devastating natural disasters that have happened throughout the history of the world. From the earliest times, scientists and inventors have studied the causes of these disasters and attempted to predict them or to make their results less destructive. Some of the innovations and discoveries they have made are cataloged here, too.

Tyrannosaurus rex fossil (65 MYA)

250 million years ago (MYA)
In the largest mass extinction in Earth's history, 90 percent of all living organisms die out. Scientists cannot find a single cause, but massive volcanic eruptions in Siberia may have altered the climate worldwide.

65 MYA
A massive asteroid or comet hits the Yucatán Peninsula, Mexico, generating a megatsunami that wipes out 50 percent of all species, including dinosaurs.

c. 2200 BCE
Records suggest that the city of Troy, in modern Turkey, was hit by a meteor shower which set fire to the city and killed most of the population.

c. 1640 BCE
The island of Santorini in the Mediterranean erupts, causing a tsunami that destroys the Minoan civilization on Crete. Many people link this event with the legend of Atlantis.

79 CE
In Italy, the eruption of Mount Vesuvius destroys the towns of Pompeii and Herculaneum.

132 CE
In China, Zhang Heng invents the first earthquake detector.

1348
Black Death, or the bubonic plague, arrives in Europe from the East. It kills 30 million people—a quarter of Europe's population.

1441
Concerned about the lives of peasants working on the land, King Sejong of Korea orders the development of a rain gauge to forecast floods and droughts.

1492–1900
Ninety percent of the Native-American population dies, many as a result of infectious diseases, such as smallpox, brought to the continent by Europeans.

1556
On January 3, the most destructive earthquake in recorded history hits Shaanxi province, China, killing 800,000 people. Many are buried alive.

1703
Edo (now Tokyo), Japan, is destroyed by an earthquake and tsunami that kills 200,000 people.

1752
Dangerous experiments with electricity by Benjamin Franklin will eventually lead to the invention of the lightning rod.

1755
Triggered by an earthquake, a tsunami hits Lisbon, Portugal, with waves 50 ft (15 m) high. It claims about 60,000 lives.

Minoan palace at Knossos (1640 BCE)

1792
An avalanche of debris from the side of Mount Unzen near Nagasaki, Japan, creates a tsunami that kills more than 14,000.

1798
English doctor Edward Jenner develops the first-ever vaccine, against smallpox.

Benjamin Franklin's lightning experiment, 1752

1815
Mount Tambora blows apart Sumbawa island, Indonesia, in the largest eruption in recorded history. The dust and gas produced affect the global climate, and 1815 becomes known as the Year Without a Summer.

1840s
Potato blight destroys potato crops throughout Europe, bringing widespread famine. In Ireland, where most of the population rely on potatoes for food, more than one million die.

1851–66
China's Yellow and Yangtze rivers flood repeatedly over the triangle of land between them known as the Rice Bowl. Up to 50 million people drown in the 15 years of flooding.

1860s
Weather-observing stations are set up around the globe. Information collected over a wide area can be compared and will be used to make accurate weather forecasts.

1864
Inspired by Swiss philanthropist Henri Dunant, the International Committee of the Red Cross, the first international aid organization, is founded in Geneva, Switzerland.

1874–76
Measles kills a third of the native population of Fiji, Polynesia. The disease has been introduced to the island by Europeans.

1882–83
German scientist Robert Koch identifies the bacteria that cause cholera and tuberculosis.

1883
Eruption of the volcanic island of Krakatau (Krakatoa), Indonesia, generates a tsunami that kills 36,000 in Java and Sumatra.

1885
British geologist John Milne invents the first modern seismograph for measuring ground tremors.

1900
In the worst local natural disaster in US history, a hurricane and storm surge kill more than 6,000 at Galveston, Texas.

1902
On May 8, Mount Pelée, Martinique, erupts. It leaves only two survivors out of 30,000 in St. Pierre, and causes a tsunami in the Caribbean.

1906
The Great San Francisco Earthquake is estimated to have killed nearly 3,000. The fires that follow burn the mostly wooden city to the ground. New buildings have to conform to earthquake safety regulations.

1908
A possible comet explodes before impact near Tunguska, in a remote region of northern Russia. The huge blast flattens 850 sq miles (2,200 sq km) of forest, but no deaths are recorded in this largely unpopulated area.

1911
On January 31, on the island of Luzon in the Philippines, the Ta'al volcano obliterates 13 villages and towns. Most of the 1,335 victims choke on ash and sulfur dioxide.

TransAmerica earthquake-proof skyscraper, San Francisco, 1972

Floods, England, 1953

1917–18
Influenza epidemic kills 25–50 million people worldwide.

1921–22
A drought and civil war devastate the region of Volga, Russia, causing widespread famine. More than 20 million people are affected.

1923
The Great Kanto Earthquake hits Tokyo, Japan, killing 140,000 people and destroying 360,000 buildings.

1930s
Droughts along with poor farming methods lead to the creation of the Dust Bowl across the US states of Kansas, Oklahoma, Texas, Colorado, and New Mexico. Famine drives 300,000 people to abandon their farms.

1931
After heavy rain, the Yangtze River in China rises to 95 ft (29 m) above its normal level, flooding large areas of the country and destroying crops. In the floods and famine that follow, about 3,700,000 people die.

1935
American Charles Richter invents the Richter scale to measure earthquake magnitude.

1946
Following a tsunami that struck Hawaii, the Pacific Tsunami Warning Center is set up in Honolulu.

1946
The United Nations International Children's Emergency Fund (UNICEF) is founded to provide emergency aid to children in case of war or natural disaster.

1953
A storm surge in the North Sea hits the Netherlands with 13-ft (4-m) waves, killing 1,800 people. It also produces 8-ft (2.5-m) waves in Essex, England, killing 300 people.

1958
Lituya Bay, Alaska, is hit by the largest local tsunami in recent history, when a massive landslide produces a wave 1,720 ft (525 m) high.

1960
In May, the largest earthquake ever recorded, measuring 9.5 on the Richter scale, hits Chile, causing tsunamis that affect Chile, Peru, Hawaii, and Japan.

1968–74
A seven-year drought occurs in the Sahel region of Africa. By 1974, 50 million people are relying on food from international aid agencies.

1970
An earthquake measuring 7.7 occurs off the coast of Peru, causing a massive avalanche and mudslide on the Nevados Huascarán Mountain, which kills 18,000 people.

1971
The worst hurricane (tropical cyclone) in history hits Bangladesh with winds up to 155 mph (250 kph) and a 25-ft (7.5-m) storm surge. The estimated death toll ranges from 300,000 to one million people.

1976
On July 28, an earthquake measuring 7.8 hits Tangshan, China, where 93 percent of the city's mud-brick houses collapse. The quake crushes 242,000 people to death.

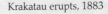

Krakatau erupts, 1883

1979
After a worldwide vaccination campaign, the WHO announces that smallpox is eradicated from all the countries.

1980
On May 18, Mount St. Helens, Washington, erupts. A successful evacuation is carried out, and only 57 lives are lost.

1984–85
An extended drought in Ethiopia and Sudan kills 450,000 people.

1985
On November 13, the eruption of Nevado del Ruiz, Colombia, causes a mudslide that covers the town of Armero with 130 ft (40 m) of mud, killing 22,800 people.

1985
An earthquake measuring 8.1 hits Mexico City, killing more than 8,000, and leaving 30,000 homeless.

1988
In Armenia, an earthquake measuring 6.9 causes newly built apartment buildings to collapse, killing 25,000.

1991
Mount Pinatubo, Philippines, erupts in June, ejecting so much debris into the atmosphere that global temperatures drop slightly for the next 15 months.

1992
In August, Hurricane Andrew strikes the Bahamas, Florida, and Louisiana, killing 65 and causing $20 billion worth of damage.

1992
In December, a tsunami with waves 86 ft (26 m) high hits the coast of Flores, Indonesia, killing 2,000 and leaving 90,000 homeless.

1993
Summer flooding on the Mississippi and Missouri rivers causes $12 billion worth of damage.

1995
In Kobe, Japan, 5,500 die as buildings collapse in an earthquake measuring 7.2.

1997
Pyroclastic flows from the Soufrière Hill inundate Plymouth, capital of Montserrat.

1997
In September, wildfires in Indonesia destroy more than 750,000 acres (300,000 hectares) of forest and bush, creating a widespread haze of pollution.

1998
Flooding in Bangladesh caused by a very strong El Niño kills 2,000 and leaves 30 million homeless.

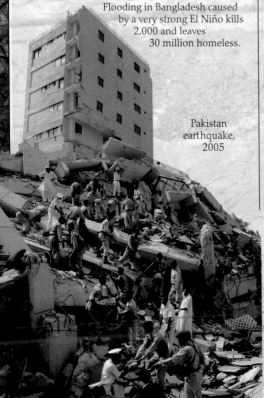

Pakistan earthquake, 2005

1998
In October, Hurricane Mitch strikes Central America, killing about 11,000 and leaving 1.5 million homeless.

1999
On May 3, a tornado outbreak occurs in Oklahoma. More than 50 tornadoes rip across the state in one day, killing over 40 people.

1999
An earthquake along Turkey's North Anatolian Fault destroys 150,000 buildings in Izmit, killing 17,000 people.

2001
In January, an earthquake in Gujarat, India, flattens 400,000 buildings, many of them poorly constructed, killing 20,000 people.

2001
On January 31, massive mudslides caused by an earthquake in El Salvador kill 265 people in the capital, San Salvador.

2002
Severe Acute Respiratory Syndrome (SARS), a previously unknown viral disease, first appears in Guandong, China.

2003
On December 27, an earthquake destroys the city of Bam, Iran, killing 26,000.

2004
On December 26, a tsunami in the Indian Ocean kills over 200,000 people.

2005
In August, the category 5 Hurricane Katrina hits the southern United States.

2005
On October 8, over 86,000 people are killed by a magnitude 7.6 earthquake in northern Pakistan and parts of Kashmir.

Tornado, Midwestern US

2008
Cyclone Nargis strikes Myanmar on May 2. Catastrophic floods kill more than 138,000.

2008
On May 12, a magnitude 8.0 earthquake kills 68,000 people in Sichuan, China.

2009
Black Saturday bushfires of February 7 sweep through Victoria, Southeastern Australia.

Health workers, Sars outbreak, 2002

2010
Up to 100,000 people die in Haiti when an earthquake strikes the most highly populated part of the country on January 12.

2010
On August 8, heavy rain triggers a mudslide that kills more than 1,470 people in Gansu province, China.

2010–2011
Queensland, Australia, suffers a series of crippling floods caused by Cyclone Tasha.

2011
Christchurch in New Zealand is struck by earthquakes in both February and June.

2011
On March 11, a massive earthquake causes a colossal tsunami that devastates the coastal regions of northeast Japan, killing at least 15,839.

Find out more

Aₗₜₕₒᵤgₕ ᵧₒᵤ ₚᵣₒbₐbₗy do not want to be around when a natural disaster is happening, you can find out more about natural disasters by visiting some of the places mentioned in this book. For example, you could investigate flood defenses at London's Thames Barrier, visit volcanic geysers in Yellowstone Park, Montana and Wyoming, or take a trip back in time in Pompeii, Italy. There is lots of information on the internet, too, including up-to-date news about the latest events.

PLACES TO VISIT

Many large cities have museums that feature in-depth exhibits about Earth's structure, the weather, and space. Check your local telephone directory, visit the library, or search the internet to find out about natural history museums in your area.

Smithsonian Institution
Washington, DC
(202) 633-1000
www.si.edu

American Museum of Natural History
New York, NY
(212) 769-5100
www.amnh.org

Field Museum
Chicago, IL
(312) 922-9410
www.fieldmuseum.org

California Academy of Sciences
San Francisco, CA
(415) 321-8000
www.calacademy.org

YELLOWSTONE
The world's first national park owes its creation to its spectacular geological features. Its geysers, bubbling mud, and hot springs are signs of a huge underground magma chamber.

Yellowstone National Park, founded in 1872

RICHTER SCALE

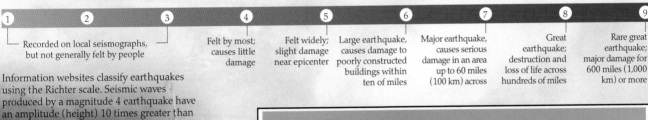

1	2	3	4	5	6	7	8	9

Recorded on local seismographs, but not generally felt by people

Felt by most; causes little damage

Felt widely; slight damage near epicenter

Large earthquake, causes damage to poorly constructed buildings within ten of miles

Major earthquake, causes serious damage in an area up to 60 miles (100 km) across

Great earthquake; destruction and loss of life across hundreds of miles

Rare great earthquake; major damage for 600 miles (1,000 km) or more

Information websites classify earthquakes using the Richter scale. Seismic waves produced by a magnitude 4 earthquake have an amplitude (height) 10 times greater than those produced by a magnitude 3 earthquake.

USEFUL WEBSITES

- **www.tsunami.org** for the Pacific Tsunami Museum
- **www.volcano.und.nodak.edu** for information about volcanoes
- **weather.noaa.gov** for the US National Weather Service
- **weather.yahoo.com** for weather forecasts anywhere in the world and information about severe weather
- **www.panda.org**, then click on "climate change" to see the Worldwide Fund for Nature's information about climate change
- **www.fema.gov** (in US) or **www.psepc.gc.ca** (in Canada) to find out about environmental dangers, such as potential floods, that exist in your area, and how to prepare for them
- **www.stormtrack.org** for information about people who track tornadoes
- **www.epa.gov/globalwarming/kids** to find out about global warming
- **www.who.int** for information on world health risks from the World Health Organization

Radar truck used by storm trackers

SAFFIR-SIMPSON SCALE
The Saffir-Simpson Scale classifies hurricanes according to the intensity of sustained windspeeds. Short gusts may reach even faster speeds, during the storm. Less than one percent of all hurricanes are classified category 5.

Category	1	2	3	4	5
Description	Weak	Moderate	Strong	Very strong	Devastating
Wind mph (kph)	75–95 (120–153)	96–110 (154–177)	111–130 (178–209)	131–155 (210–249)	156+ (250+)
Storm surge ft (m)	4–5 (1.2–1.5)	6–8 (1.6–2.4)	9–12 (2.5–3.7)	13–18 (3.8–5.5)	18+ (5.5+)
Damage	Minimal: some tree damage	Moderate: major damage to mobile homes; roofs damaged	Extensive: mobile homes destroyed; large trees blown down	Extreme: small buildings lose roofs; most windows blown in	Catastrophic: roofs of many larger buildings lost; major storm surges

Glossary

ACID RAIN Rain made more acidic by air pollution from vehicle exhausts and emissions from factories.

AFTERSHOCK A smaller tremor that comes after the main shock of an earthquake. These aftershocks may continue for months.

AIR MASS A body of air with a fairly uniform temperature that may stretch over thousands of miles within the troposphere.

ATMOSPHERE The layer of gases that surrounds the Earth.

AVALANCHE A large mass of snow sliding down a mountainside.

BACTERIA (singular bacterium) Microscopic single-celled organisms that lack a nucleus. Some can cause disease.

BORE A giant wave created by an exceptionally high tide that rushes up low-lying rivers.

BUOY A float anchored in water, usually to mark a position. Ocean-monitoring devices can be attached to buoys that can transmit information to satellites.

CARBON A nonmetallic element that occurs in the form of graphite, diamond, and charcoal and in many compounds.

CLIMATE The regular pattern of weather in a particular region.

CRATER A bowl-shaped depression at the mouth of a volcano or caused by the impact of a meteorite.

CRUST The Earth's thin rocky outer layer.

CUMULONIMBUS CLOUD A towering white or gray cloud that may bring thunderstorms or hail.

DROUGHT A long period with little or no rainfall.

DUST DEVIL A small twisting wind that lifts dust and debris into the air.

EARTHQUAKE A series of vibrations in the Earth's crust, caused by movement at a fault in or between tectonic plates.

EL NIÑO A change in atmospheric and ocean conditions that causes warm water currents in the Pacific Ocean to flow east instead of west. El Niño occurs every few years and can disrupt the weather around the world.

EMBANKMENT A bank of soil or stone, often used to protect an area from flooding.

ENVIRONMENT The conditions and surroundings in which something exists.

EPICENTER The point on the Earth's surface directly above the focus of an earthquake.

EPIDEMIC An outbreak of a contagious disease that spreads rapidly.

ERUPTION An outpouring of hot gases, lava, and other material from a volcano.

EVACUATION An organized departure of residents from an area threatened by disaster.

FAULT A fracture in the Earth's crust along which rocks have moved relative to one another. Transform faults occur where two tectonic plates slide past one another.

Crater of Mount Vesuvius, Italy

FLASH FLOOD A flood that occurs suddenly after heavy rain.

FLOOD An overflow of water onto ground that is normally dry.

FLOOD DEFENSES Structures such as dams, embankments, levees, and sluices that are designed to redirect floodwaters to prevent land from flooding.

FLOOD PLAIN An area of flat land around a river where the river naturally floods.

FOCUS A point within the Earth's crust where an earthquake originates.

FOSSIL FUEL A fuel such as coal or oil that is derived from the remains of once living organisms buried beneath the ground.

Aialik Glacier, Alaska

FRONT The forward moving edge of an air mass. A cold front is the leading edge of a cold air mass, and a warm front is the leading edge of a warm air mass.

GLACIER A mass of year-round ice and snow that is capable of flowing slowly downhill. The largest glaciers are the Antarctic and Greenland ice sheets.

GLOBAL WARMING A gradual increase in average temperature worldwide.

GROUNDWATER Water that collects in, or flows through, rocks beneath Earth's surface.

HABITAT The natural home of a living organism.

HAILSTONE A hard pellet of ice that falls from a cumulonimbus thundercloud during a hailstorm.

HOT SPOT A site of volcanic activity far from the edges of the tectonic plates caused by magma rising from the mantle.

HURRICANE A violent storm bringing powerful twisting winds and torrential rain. Hurricanes are known as cyclones in the Indian Ocean and typhoons in the Pacific Ocean.

Lava flowing on Mount Etna, Italy

ICE AGE A period of time when ice sheets cover a large part of the Earth's surface.

IRRIGATION A system for supplying farmland with water by means of channels.

LANDSLIDE A large mass of rock or soil that slides down a hillside or breaks away from a cliff.

LAVA Molten rock that erupts from a volcano. When this material is underground it is called magma.

LEVEE A natural or artificial embankment that prevents a river from overflowing.

LIGHTNING The visible flash that occurs during a thunderstorm when electricity is discharged between a cloud and the ground or between two clouds.

MAGMA Molten rock beneath the Earth's surface. Above the ground, it is called lava.

Rickshaw drivers ride through monsoon floods in Guwahati, India

METEORITE A piece of solid material that has traveled from space, through the Earth's atmosphere, and landed on Earth.

METEOROLOGIST A scientist who studies the weather.

MOLTEN Melted to form a hot liquid.

MONSOON A seasonal wind that, when it blows from the southwest, brings heavy summer rains to southern Asia.

OZONE LAYER The layer of gas in the stratosphere that helps protect the Earth from the Sun's harmful radiation.

PANDEMIC An outbreak of disease that spreads to a vast number of people over a wide area.

PYROCLASTIC FLOW A fast-flowing and destructive outpouring of hot ash, rock, and gases from a volcano.

RADAR A system for detecting distant objects by means of reflected radio waves, to determine their size, position, and movement. Radar can be used to detect a developing tornado inside a storm cloud.

RICHTER SCALE A scale used for measuring the intensity of earthquakes, with 9+ indicating the strongest tremors.

SAFFIR-SIMPSON SCALE A scale used to measure the intensity of hurricanes. Category 5 indicates the most severe hurricanes.

SATELLITE An object that orbits a planet. Artificial satellites in orbit around the Earth are used to monitor the weather, ground movements, and changes in sea level.

SEISMIC Caused by an earthquake.

SEISMOGRAM A record of seismic activity on paper or computer produced by a seismograph.

SEISMOGRAPH A device for detecting, recording, and measuring ground tremors.

SLUICE A manmade channel with a gate for regulating water flow, used to redirect excess water in order to prevent flooding.

SMOG Fog polluted with smoke.

SONAR A system for detecting underwater objects and surfaces by means of reflected sound waves.

Supercell cloud

STORM SURGE An unusually high tide produced by the eye of a hurricane.

STRATOSPHERE The layer of the Earth's atmosphere above the troposphere, where the ozone layer is found.

SUNSPOT A dark area that appears on the surface of the Sun where magnetic forces hold the light back.

SUPERCELL CLOUD A huge storm cloud that may produce a tornado.

TECTONIC PLATE One of about 20 pieces that make up the Earth's crust. The parts of the plates that carry the continents are denser and thicker than the parts beneath the oceans.

THUNDER The sound of air expanding rapidly when it is heated by lightning.

TORNADO A spinning wind that appears as a dark, funnel-shaped cloud reaching down to the ground.

TREMOR A shaking or vibrating movement.

TRIBUTARY A river or stream that flows into a larger one.

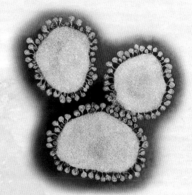

Coronavirus particles

TROPOSPHERE The layer of the atmosphere closest to the Earth's surface where all weather happens.

TSUNAMI A fast-moving ocean wave, or series of waves, generated by tectonic movements or by an object impacting the water's surface.

VENT An opening in a volcano through which lava or volcanic gases flow.

VIRUS An infectious agent comprising a microscopic package of chemicals surrounded by a protein coat. Viruses invade living cells and usually destroy them in order to reproduce.

VOLCANO An opening in the crust of the Earth through which lava escapes.

VOLCANOLOGIST A scientist who studies volcanoes.

VORTEX A tightly spiraling mass of liquid or gas. The center of a hurricane and a tornado is a vortex.

WATERSPOUT A tornado that occurs over water, producing a column of spinning mist and spray.

WAVE CREST The highest point of a wave.

WAVE TROUGH The lowest point of a wave.

Index

ABC

acid rain 57, 70
aftershocks 11, 70
aid organizations 22, 49, 66, 67
AIDS 58, 59, 60, 61, 65
air masses 32, 33, 34, 42, 70
air pressure 36, 37, 38
Andrew, Hurricane 38–39, 68
Antarctic 54
Aral Sea 48
Arctic sea ice 54
ash, volcanic 28, 29, 32, 66
Asian tsunami (2004) 15, 18–19, 22–23, 24, 64, 68
asteroids 14, 16, 17, 62, 63, 66, 67
atmosphere 32–33, 36, 56, 57, 64, 70
avalanches 30, 65, 66
bacteria 58, 60, 67, 70
Bam earthquake 12, 68
bird flu 62
bores 17, 70
boundaries, tectonic 9
buildings, quake-proof 12, 67
Canary Islands 62, 63
CFCs 56
cholera 58, 60, 67
Christchurch earthquake 68
cinder cone volcanoes 27
cliffs 31
climate 32, 70
climate change 54–55, 66
clouds 32, 34, 35, 42
cold, common 58, 59
cones, volcanic 27, 28
continents 8, 65
coral reefs 55, 57
core, Earth's 8
cores, ice 55
crop failures 48, 49, 58, 59
crust, Earth's 8, 9, 26, 70
Cumbre Vieja ridge 63
cyclones 36, 39, 68

DE

dams 45, 46, 47
debris flows 31
deforestation 50, 51, 56–57
desertification 57
deserts 33, 48
dinosaurs 54, 63, 66
diseases 7, 58–61, 62, 65
dogs 13, 22, 30
Doppler radars 43, 45
dormant volcanoes 26
droughts 7, 48–49, 50, 64, 67, 70
dust bowls 49, 67
dust devils 43, 70
dust storms 33
Earth
atmosphere 32–33, 70
climate change 54–55, 66
natural workings 6, 8–9
orbit and tilt 55
earthquakes 6, 8, 9, 10–13, 62, 64, 66, 67, 68, 70
and tsunamis 14–15, 16, 20, 22–23, 24
El Niño 37, 47, 65, 70
epicenters 10, 18, 70
epidemics 60–61, 67, 68, 70
evacuations 7, 12, 21, 28, 40, 41, 47, 50, 64
eyes/eye walls 36, 37

F

famines 48–49, 66
faults/fault lines 9, 10, 15, 25, 70
fires 12, 17, 50–53
fish stocks 57
flash floods 44, 45, 70
fleas 58
flood defenses 45, 70
flood plains 44, 46, 70
floodgates 24, 45
floods 21, 36, 40–41, 44–47, 66, 67, 68, 70
Floyd, Hurricane 38
foreshocks 11
forest fires 7, 50–53, 64, 68
fossil fuels 54, 56, 57, 64, 70
Fran, Hurricane 37
Franklin, Benjamin 66
frontal wedging 34
fronts (weather) 33, 70
Fukushima power plant 20–21, 22
fulgurites 35
fungi 58, 59
future disasters 62–63

GHI

geologists 55
Georges, Hurricane 39
geothermal energy 65
glaciers 45, 70
global warming 54, 55, 70
Great Kanto earthquake 67
Great Storm of 1987 39
groundwater 48, 70
habitats 54, 70
hailstones 35, 65, 70
Haiti earthquake 10, 68
health education 60, 61
heatwaves 50, 70
helicopters 30, 52–53
HIV 61
hospital infections 61
hot spots 26, 70
humidity 32
hurricane hunters 38
hurricanes 36–41, 64, 65, 67, 68, 69, 70
hygiene 60, 61
ice ages 63, 64, 70
ice cores 55
ice sheets 54, 55
ice storms 33
infections 58–61, 62, 65
influenza 60, 62–63, 67
islands, volcanic 9, 26
isobars 33
Ivan, Hurricane 36

JKL

Japanese tsunami (2011) 20–21, 23, 65, 68
Katrina, Hurricane 40–41, 68
Kilauea volcano 6, 9
Kobe earthquake 12–13, 68
Koch, Robert 67
Krakatau volcano 67
landslides 14, 16, 17, 30–31, 70
lava 6, 9, 26, 27, 70
Leeuwenhoek, Anton van 58
levees 40, 47, 70
lightning 34–35, 50, 64, 65, 70
lightning conductors 34, 66
Lisbon earthquake 6, 66
Lituya Bay tsunami 16, 67
local tsunamis 14, 16, 17

M

magma 9, 26, 62, 65, 69, 70
malaria 7, 58, 61
mass extinctions 63, 66
Mauna Kea volcano 27
Mayan civilization 46
Mayon volcano 7
measles 60, 67
megatsunamis 62, 63
mesocyclones 42
mesosphere 32
meteorites 14, 71
meteorologists 34, 35, 38, 71
microorganisms 58
microscopes 58–59
Milne, John 67
Minoan civilization 66
Mitch, Hurricane 68
monitoring and predicting
avalanches 30
climate change 55
earthquakes 10, 11, 18, 24
hurricanes 37, 38–39
Near Earth Objects 63
tornadoes 43
tsunamis 24–25
volcanic eruptions 27, 28
weather 33, 34, 35, 45, 66
monsoon 44, 47, 52, 71
mosquitoes 7, 60, 61
Mount Etna 28–29
Mount Fuji 26
Mount Pelée 14, 67
Mount Pinatubo 29, 32, 68
Mount St. Helens 28, 65, 67
Mount Spurr 32
Mount Tambora 66
Mount Vesuvius 29, 62, 66
MRSA 61
mudslides 30, 67, 68

NOP

Nargis, Cyclone 39, 68
natural resources 56, 57
Near Earth Objects (NEO) 62, 63
New Orleans floods 40–41
Nile River 44
Noah's ark 46
nuclear disasters 20–21, 22, 23
oceanic plates 9, 15, 20, 64
optical telescopes 63
ozone layer 56, 64, 71
Pakistan earthquake (2005) 6, 68
pandemics 60, 61, 62, 71
Paricutin volcano 27
plague 58, 60, 64
polar regions 54
pollution 52, 54, 55, 64, 65, 68
Pompeii 29, 62, 66, 69
population 62
potato blight 59, 66
prevailing winds 33
pyroclastic flows 29, 71

R

radars 11, 43, 71
radiation levels 21, 22, 64
rainclouds 34
rainfall 31, 34, 36, 37, 44, 48, 57, 64
rainforests 50, 51
rats 60
recovery, post-disaster 22–23
refugee camps 22, 49, 58
rescue teams 13, 21, 22–23, 30, 31, 41, 46, 47, 52–53, 65
Richter scale 10, 67, 69, 71
Ring of Fire 64
Rita, Hurricane 41
rivers, flooding 44–47
rockfalls 31

S

Saffir-Simpson scale 69, 71
Sahara Desert 48, 64
San Andreas Fault 10
San Francisco earthquake (1906) 67
SARS 68
satellites 25, 32, 34, 36, 37, 38, 39, 50, 71
Scarborough cliff fall 31
seismic waves 10, 69
seismograms 18, 71
seismographs 11, 24, 67, 71
shelters, emergency 13, 22, 40
shield cone volcanoes 27
sluices 45, 71
slumping 31
smallpox 58, 59, 60, 66, 67
smog 52, 56, 64, 65, 71
smokejumpers 53
snow 30
soil 26, 51, 53, 64
soil creep 31
solar flares 64
sonar 25, 71
Soufrière Hills volcano 14
storm chasers 43
storm surges 37, 38, 40, 67, 71
storms 33–43
stratosphere 32, 71
stratovolcanoes 27
subduction 9
Sun 6, 32, 33, 34, 36, 54, 55
sunspots 64, 71
supercell clouds 42, 71
supervolcanoes 62
Surtsey 26
swine flu 62

TU

Ta'al volcano 67
tectonic plates 8–9, 14, 20, 64, 71
tectonic tsunamis 14–15, 16, 17
temperatures 27, 32, 36, 37, 52, 54, 55
Thames Barrier 45, 69
thermal images 50
thermosphere 32
Three Gorges Dam 45, 46
thunder 34, 64, 71
thunderheads 42
thunderstorms/clouds 32, 33, 34–35
tidal bores 17
Tornado Alley 42
tornadoes 42–43, 64, 65, 68, 71
transform faults 9
tropical storms 36, 37
troposphere 32, 71
tsunamis 6, 9, 14–25, 62, 63, 64, 66, 67, 71
tuberculosis 58, 67
twisters 42–43
typhoons 36, 65
unnatural disasters 56–57

VWY

vaccinations 60
Victoria floods (2010) 47
viruses 58, 59, 62–63, 71
volcanoes 6, 7, 8, 9, 14, 26–29, 62, 63, 64, 65, 66, 67, 69, 71
vortex 43, 71
warning systems 24, 25, 30, 37, 45, 67
water
and disease 58, 60
supplies 48
waterspouts 43, 71
waves 16, 18, 71
weather 6, 32, 33, 34–43
weather planes 34, 35, 38
wells 48–49
wildfires 50–3, 68
winds 33, 36–43
Yellowstone National Park 26, 62, 69
Yucatan Peninsula meteorite 63, 66

Acknowledgments

Dorling Kindersley would like to thank Stewart J. Wild for proofreading and Helen Peters for indexing.

The publisher would like to thank the following for their kind permission to reproduce their photographs:
(Key: a-above; b-below/bottom; c-center; f-far; l-left; r-right; t-top)

1 Science Photo Library: NOAA. **2 Corbis:** Jim Reed (br); Roger Ressmeyer (tr). **2 Getty Images:** Jimin Lai/AFP (br). **2 Rex Features:** HXL (tl). **3 DK Images:** Courtesy of Glasgow Museum (tr); Courtesy of the Museo Archeologico Nazionale di Napoli (bl). **Photolibrary.com:** Warren Faidley/OSF (tl). **Science Photo Library:** Planetary Visions Ltd (cr); Zephyr (br). **4 www.bridgeman.co.uk:** The Great Wave of Kanagawa, from 'Thirty six views of Mount Fuji', c.1831, colour woodblock print (detail) by Hokusai, Katsushika, Tokyo Fuji Art Museum, Tokyo, Japan (bl). **Corbis:** Dan Lamont (br). **DK Images:** (tl); Michael Zabe CONACULTA-INAH-MEX. Authorized reproduction by the Instituto Nacional de Antropologia. **Rex Features:** Masatoshi Okauchi (cr), **Science Photo Library:** NASA (tr). **5 Corbis:** Alfio Scigliano/Sygma. **6 Corbis:** Noburu Hashimoto (b). **Getty Images:** Jim Sugar/Science Faction (cr). **Science Photo Library:** (tr); Planetary Visions Ltd (tl). 7 **Corbis:** Frans Lanting (tr). **Getty Images:** Aaron McCoy/Lonely Planet Images (cl); Andres Hernandez/Getty Images News (b). **Science Photo Library:** Eye of Science (cr). **8 DK Images:** Courtesy of the Natural History Museum, London (tl). **9 Corbis:** (cl), (c); Kevin Schafer (cr). **Rob Francis:** (b). **10 www.bridgeman.co.uk:** The Great Wave of Kanagawa, from 'Thirty six views of Mount Fuji', c.1831, colour woodblock print (detail) by Hokusai, Katsushika, Tokyo Fuji Art Museum, Tokyo, Japan (tl). **Corbis:** Academy of Natural Sciences of Philadelphia (tr); Reuters (br). **Science Photo Library:** Stephen & Donna O'Meara (cl). **11 Corbis:** David de la Paz (t). **11 Science Photo Library:** Digital Globe, Eurimage (tl); (tr). **12 Corbis:** Lloyd Cluff (b). **Science Photo Library:** George Bernard (c). **12–13** Tony Friedkin/Sony Pictures Classics/ZUMA. **13 Corbis:** (cr). **Empics Ltd:** AP (b). **Associate Professor Ted Bryant, Associate Dean of Science, University of Wollongong** (t). **14 Corbis:** Dadang Tri/Reuters (tl). **Empics Ltd:** AP (br). **Rex Features:** SIPA (b). **15 Empics Ltd:** (cr); Karim Khamzin/AP (b). **Panos Pictures:** Tim A. Hetherington (cl). **Reuters:** Amateur Video Grab (t). **16 Corbis:** Thomas Thompson/WFP/Handout/Reuters (cl). **Getty Images:** Jimin Lai/AFP (b). **Panos Pictures:** Dieter Telemans (tr). **16–17 Corbis:** Babu/Reuters (c). **17 Corbis:** Bazuki Muhammas/Reuters (bl); Yuriko Nakao (tr). **Rex Features:** RSR (br). **18 Empics Ltd:** Wang Xiaochuan/AP (tr). **Rex Features:** HXL (tl); Nick Cornish (NCH) (t); SS/Keystone USA (KUS) (cl). **18-19 Corbis:** Chaiwat Subprasom/Reuters (b). **19 Rex Features:** IJO (br); Roy Garner (c). **20-21 Getty Images:** JIJI Press / AFP (b). **20 Getty Images:** Yasuyoshil Chiba / AFP (tl). NOAA: (tr). **21 Corbis:** Tepco / Xinhua Press (tl); Kyodo / Xinhua Press (tr). Getty Images: DigitalGlobe (c); Yomiuri Shimbun / AFP (br). **20 Getty Images:** Getty Images News (b). **Panos Pictures:** Dean Chapman (tl). **Rex Features:** Masatoshi Okauchi (tr). **21 Corbis:** Chaiwat Subprasom/Reuters (r). **Empics Ltd:** Lucy Pemoni/AP (cr). **Getty Images:** Getty Images News (cl). **Science Photo Library:** David Ducros (tl); US Geological Survey (b). **22 Corbis:** STR / epa (tr). **23 Alamy Images:** James P. Jones (br). **Getty Images:** Kazuhiro Nogi / AFP (t). **22 Corbis:** Reuters (br). **Science Photo Library:** Georg Gerster (cl). **23 Corbis:** Owen Franken (t). **DK Images:** Science Museum, London (cr). **Science Photo Library:** NASA (bl); Zephyr (br). **24 Corbis:** Kurt Stier (cl); Patrick Robert/Sygma (tr); Ryan Pyle (bl). **24–25 Rex Features:** Sipa Press (b). **25 Corbis:** Andrea Comas/Reuters (br); Michael S. Yamashita (tl). **26 Corbis:** Jose Fuste Raga (tr). **© Michael Holford:** (tl). **FLPA—Images of Nature:** S. Jonasson (bl). **26–27 Science Photo Library:** Bernhard Edmaier (b). **27 Corbis:** Reuters (cr). **Science Photo Library:** Mauro Fermariello (cl). **28 Corbis:** Gary Braasch (tl); Roger Ressmeyer (cl). **28–29 Corbis:** Alfio Scigliano/Sygma (bc). **29 www.bridgeman.co.uk:** Private Collection, Archives Charmet (cl). **Corbis:** Alberto Garcia (t). **DK Images:** Courtesy of the Museo Archeologico Nazionale di Napoli (br). **Empics Ltd:** Itsuo Inouye/AP Photo (cr). 30 Corbis: John Van Hasselt (cr); Lowell Georgia (tr); S.P. Gillette (cl). **Getty Images:** Vedros & Associates/The Image Bank (tl). **Science Photo Library:** Mark Clarke (br). **31 Corbis:** Jonathan Blair (cl); Reuters (bl), (bc). **Robert Harding Picture Library:** Tony Waltham (br). **32 Alamy Images:** Andrew Parker (br). **32–33 Science Photo Library:** NASA (c). **33 Corbis:** Christopher Morris (bl). **US Marine Corps:** Gunnery Sgt. Shannon Arledge (br). **34 Science Photo Library:** Jean-Loup Charmet (tl). **34–35 Science Photo Library:** Kent Wood (c). **35 Corbis:** George Hall (t). **FLPA—Images of Nature:** Jim Reed (fbr). **Science Photo Library:** Jim Reed (cb); Peter Menzel (c). **36 Corbis:** Frances Litman / All Canada Photos (tr). **36 Science Photo Library:** Colin Cuthbert (tr); NOAA (b). **37 Photolibrary.com:** Warren Faidley/OSF (b); Warren Faidley/OSF (tr). **Science Photo Library:** Jim Reed (c); NOAA (tl). **38 Corbis:** Reuters (b). **Science Photo Library:** Chris Sattlberger (cl), (cr) **38–39 Science Photo Library:** NASA/Goddard Space Flight Center (t). **39 Corbis:** epa (tr). **39 Empics Ltd:** Dave Martin/AP (br). **Getty Images:** Ed Pritchard/Stone (cl). **FLPA—Images of Nature:** (tr). **40 Corbis:** Irwin Thompson/Dallas Morning News (bl); Smiley N. Pool/Dallas Morning News (cl); Vincent Laforet/Pool/Reuters (br) **41 Corbis:** Irwin Thompson/Dallas Morning News (tr); Ken Cedeno (tl); Michael Ainsworth/Dallas Morning News (br). **40–41 Science Photo Library:** NOAA (c). **42 Photolibrary. com:** Warren Faidley/OSF (c), (bl), (bc), (br). **43 Photolibrary.com:** Warren Faidley/OSF (cl). **Corbis:** (c). **Science Photo Library:** J.G. Golden (cr); Jim Reed (bl); Mary Beth Angelo (tr). **44 Getty Images:** AFP (tr). **44–45 Corbis:** Reuters (bc). **45 Corbis:** Jim Reed (bc), (br); Reuters (tl); Tom Bean (tr). **46 DK Images:** Michael Zabe CONACULTA-INAH-MEX. Authorized reproduction by the Instituto Nacional de Antropologia (tr). **46–47 Corbis:** Reuters (b). **47 Corbis:** Brooks Kraft (tr); Rafiqur Rahman/Reuters (br); Romeo Ranoco/Reuters (c). Magnum: Philip Jones-Griffiths (tl). **47 Getty Images:** Scott Barbour (c).**48 Corbis: Despotovic Dusko/Sygma** (cl). **Magnum:** Steve McCurry (bl). **Science Photo Library:** Novosti Photo Library (tr). **48–49 Corbis:** Reuters (cb). 48 Corbis: Dusko Despotovic / Sygma (cl).**49 Corbis:** Howard Davies (br). **Getty Images:** Time Life Pictures (tl). **Photolibrary. com:** Sarah Puttnam/Index Stock Imagery (tr). **49 Getty Images:** John Moore (cr). **50 Corbis:** Polypix, Eye Ubiquitous (tl); Stephenie Maze (bl). **FLPA—Images of Nature:** Ben Van den Brink/Foto Natura (cl). **Science Photo Library:** NASA (tr). **50–51 Corbis:** Jonathan Blair. 50-51 Getty Images: The AGE / Fairfax Media (b). **51 Corbis:** Douglas Faulkner (tl); Ed Kashi (tr). **52 NASA:** (cl). **Panos Pictures:** Paul Lowe (b). **52–53 Corbis:** Steven K. Doi/ZUMA. **53 Corbis:** Dan Lamont (b). **Panos Pictures:** Dean Sewell (c), (t). **54 Getty Images:** Highlights for Children / Photolibrary (tr). **54 Science Photo Library:** (t); NASA (cl), (cr). **54–55 Corbis:** Hans Strand. **55 Science Photo Library:** Alexis Rosenfield (cl); British Antarctic Survey (cr). **56 Science Photo Library:** BSIG, M.I.G./BAEZA (bl); David Hay Jones (tl); NASA (tr). **56–57 Getty Images:** Steven Wienberg/Photographer's Choice. **57 FLPA—Images of Nature:** Norbert Wu/Minden Pictures (cr). **Magnum:** Jean Gaumy (tl). **Science Photo Library:** Simon Fraser (br). **Still Pictures:** W. Ming (tr). **58 Empics Ltd:** David Guttenfelder/AP (bl); Jordan Peter/PA (cl). **Science Photo Library:** John Burbridge tr. **58–59 Science Photo Library:** Colin Cuthbert. **59 Science Photo Library:** Andrew Syred (tr); Astrid & Hanns-Frieder Michler (tl); Eye of Science (cr). **60 Empics Ltd:** John Moore/AP (bl). **Eye Ubiquitous:** Hutchison (br). **Science Photo Library:** James King-Holmes (tl). **61 Corbis:** Erik de Castro/Reuters (br); Pallava Bagla (t). **Science Photo Library:** AJ Photo/Hop Americain (c); Andy Crump, TDR, WHO (tr); CDC (cl); NIBSC (bc). **62 Corbis:** Claro Cortes IV/Reuters (bc); Jeff Vanuga (t); Roger Ressmeyer (bl). **Science Photo Library:** CDC/C. Goldsmith/J. Katz/S. Zaki (cr). **63 Corbis:** Roger Ressmeyer (tr). **Science Photo Library:** NASA (tl), (b). **64 Corbis:** Reuters (br); Sally A. Morgan, Ecoscene (l); Ted Soqui (tr). **64–65 Science Photo Library:** NASA, background. **65 Corbis:** Reuters (l); Vinve Streano (br). **Science Photo Library:** Russell Kightley (tr). **66 Corbis:** Gianni Dagli Orti (bl). **The Art Archive:** (tr). **66 Science Photo Library:** Mehau Kulyk (tl); Photo Researchers (cr). **66–67 Rob Francis:** background. **66–67 Getty Images:** Fraser Hall/Robert Harding World Imagery (bc). **67 Photolibrary.com:** Mary Plage/OSF (cra). **Corbis:** Bettmann (crb). **Science Photo Library:** Bettmann (tc). **68 Corbis:** Faisal Mahmood/Reuters (bl); Reuters (cr). **Science Photo Library:** Eric Nguyen/Jim Reed Photography (tr). **68–69 Rob Francis:** background. **69 Corbis:** Jim Reed (bl). **70 Science Photo Library:** Jeremy Bishop (cr). 71 **Corbis:** Reuters (t). **Science Photo Library:** Dr Linda Stannard, UCT (cr); Jim Reed (bc).

Wall chart: Corbis: Arno Balzarini / epa (fclb), Alberto Garcia (bl), Rafiqur Rahman / Reuters (c), Roger Ressmeyer (br), Wave (cr); **Dorling Kindersley**: Aberdeen Fire Department, Maryland (fcr); **Getty Images**: Jeff Hunter / The Image Bank (tr) / (Background), Tom Pfeiffer / VolcanoDiscovery / Photographer's Choice (b), JIJI Press / AFP (cl); **NASA**: Scientific Visualization Studio Collection (cr) / (hurricane); **NASA Goddard Space Flight Center** : (crb); **U.S. Geological Survey**: Walter Mooney (cla); **Courtesy of U.S. Army**: Capt. Daniel A. Hill, 49th PAD (clb), Tech. Sgt. James B. Pritchett (tr)

Jacket: *Front:* **Alamy Images**: George and Monserrate Schwartz (tc). **Corbis**: Joseph Sohm / Visions of America (tl). **Press Association Images**: Dave Martin / AP (b). *Back:* **Dorling Kindersley**: National Maritime Museum, London (br); Ted Taylor—modelmaker (bc). **Science Photo Library**: NOAA (c).

All other images © Dorling Kindersley.
For further information, see: **www.dkimages.com**